A MAN LIKE YOU AND ME

A SUPERNATURAL ADVENTURE STORY

Paul Joel

ISBN: 979-8-89216-040-7 (Paperback)
        979-8-89216-041-4 (E-book)

Library of Congress Control Number: 2024918887

Published By:

Albany, NY
https://pauljoelbook.com/

Publisher Provider:

TABLE OF CONTENTS

CHAPTER 1

MUNICH

"MR. JAMES PAUL, THIS is your wake-up call. The tour bus to Neuschwanstein Castle will be leaving from the train station in exactly one hour," announced the efficient German clerk.

I had just arrived in Munich last night and found this boarding house three blocks from the train station. It was clean and inexpensive. It's difficult to explain why I was in Munich. I had three weeks of vacation time and a Eurail pass to board any train with second-class seats, but why visit Munich again? Five years ago, I stopped in Munich to visit the Dachau Concentration camp and left Germany within 24 hours. I hate Germans. I hate this city. After growing up in New York City, I despise most cities. Munich was where the Nazi Party was founded. It was the good Catholic, fun-loving Bavarian Christians who made Hitler a success. Of course, now, 37 years after World War II, there are no Nazis in Germany, with the exception that you see a few of them celebrating Hitler's birthday on the twentieth of April each year. At one time, almost fifty percent of the adult population voted Hitler into power. As an American who has no use for any ethnic minority or religious group – that should just about include everybody – there was absolutely no reason to get off the train and visit Munich.

"Thank you. May I leave my backpack with you until I return from King Ludwig's Castle?" I asked after checking out.

"That would be no problem. I'll put it in this closet. You can pick it up any time you want.

My schedule was to sleep on the train to Vienna that evening, thereby saving the cost of a hotel room. After all, Hitler went from Vienna, where he was unemployed and learned to hate Jews, to Munich, where he eventually became a success. With my luck, I'll probably go from Munich as a physician to Vienna and become an unemployed bum. I tried a concentration camp; now I'll visit a castle. That should cover seeing Germany.

The tour guide was probably a frustrated ex SS officer. Every time the bus passed the odor of manure, he would comment about the fresh country air. Again, it was difficult to understand why I left my private practice of almost two years to go off on this vacation to Europe. I don't like people, nor do I care to see any of the things they made. I have no friends and consider the world to be a large sewer. That's why it's important to be able to swim with your head out of the water. People are friendly and helpful as long as you don't need them, and they don't have to go out of their way. In New York City, you just hope that you're not the next murder, rape, or assault victim. Patients are tolerated only because they pay a fee.

Starting with elementary school, I disliked every institution with which I was ever associated. What was there to like about school? Usually, a very boring teacher would assign work and then grade you. The fundamental skill for success at school was to tolerate total boredom without annoying anyone. I mastered that skill in first grade. By third grade, I could vegetate in a semi-stuporous state for hours without annoying anyone. A problem would arise when I was pushed to my limit when a particularly sadistic teacher would attempt to increase classroom participation by leading a discussion. Then I would be subjected to students who were even more boring than the teacher. Except for reading, writing, and arithmetic, I never learned anything useful in school.

The only thing worse than school was working in a hospital. As a medical student, I was introduced to compassion for the sick when I accompanied an intern to the emergency room during my first evening on-call. As I approached the patient, I heard the chief resident scream at a drug addict, our new admission, "The sooner you die, the better off I'll be." The resident was complaining about the revolving door nature of the patient's multiple admissions. He was suggesting in a crude way that when the patient presented for his fifteenth admission in the last two years, he might do it during the daytime and not at 3 AM. You learned to treat the patient and help him survive the acute illness. Then he would return to the lifestyle that had contributed to his illness, and soon he would be in need of further treatment. As a physician, you always treated the acute illness, the tree, and limited yourself to that picture. You had to develop a blind spot. Never look at the whole picture, the forest, because it is too depressing. People don't change. They never change. They don't wake up one morning and become happy, well-adjusted, and normal after they had previously been morose, bitter, and miserable. People don't change, but they are changed. Events change the person.

In the hospital, you witness the great events of life that change people – birth, sickness, and death. When a couple has their first child, the parents are forever changed. They are sentenced to parenthood until death. Sickness can be so overwhelming that for many patients, the illness and treatment forever dominate their lives. How many times have I listened to a patient tell me about his heart attack and open heart surgery? His disease and therapy combine to produce a new illness. Previously the patient was a human being with a little chest pain. After surgery, he turned into some drone, gesticulating spasmodically about cholesterol, fats, operative procedures, and personal exercise programs. Pass me the burgers and fries and give me death without surgery.

No wonder I hated working in the hospital. It's the institution of death. The main function of hospitals is to keep death out of the patient's view. That's why every hospital has a morgue. A complicated emergency paramedical system has developed to scoop up any acutely ill person and immediately transport him to a hospital where he can die in peace. Most Americans are pronounced dead in the hospital or nursing home, a chronic hospital specializing in the care of the elderly living dead. As soon as a patient dies, there is a mad scramble. I've never seen a floor nurse move more quickly than to isolate the dead body, cover it and get it off the ward before anyone realizes that the hospital is the house of death. Conversely, the nurses always takes their time when the patient requests medication for the relief of pain. Then comes the important ritual of documenting the cause of death and the exact time of death. The physician then climbs to the altar at this point because only he can declare the patient dead. He's a glorified baseball umpire. Never mind where the ball was pitched; if the umpire calls it a strike, then it's a strike. If the ball was pitched right down the center of the strike zone and the umpire called it a ball, it was a ball. The same thing happened with doctors and death. A nurse might note on the medical chart that the patient had no blood pressure, no pulse, no response to painful stimuli, and the pupils were fixed and dilated. There was no sign of respiration. In fact, the patient was cold and stone dead. Rigor mortis was setting in because the patient had, in fact, died in the x-ray department days ago. However, the patient is still alive until pronounced dead by the physician. In the old days, people were a lot smarter. Most people could identify a dead person. If you kicked him and he didn't move for forty-eight hours, chances were he was dead. Now the criteria have changed. It's more complicated. That's why physicians specialize. It's so difficult to differentiate the people from the plants.

The worst part of being a physician was dealing with patients before they died. Female patients were the worst! Men were fine. You could talk to them. You could explain to him how it was necessary to remove his left ear and stuff it into his right nostril to improve his vision. Usually, the man would acknowledge his ignorance of medical physiology and resign himself to the physician's expertise and let me decide what was in his best interest. The female was used to running the household; she would decide. First, she wanted a list of every test, every drug, and every condition that might have some relationship to any of the seventy-five symptoms about which she was complaining. After canceling a few of the tests I had scheduled and seeing every physician within a twenty-mile radius who did not have the good sense to throw her out of the office, a momentary course of action would be agreed upon. This she would change the next day.

"We are stopping at this church for twenty-three minutes. You may get coffee across the street but make certain you return to the bus by 10:37. The bus will leave promptly at 10:39," announced the tour guide.

Well, another church to visit. I didn't know this was on the schedule. It was really a prolonged coffee and bathroom stop. I hate churches. God does not exist. Man invented Him to attempt to make sense of this disgusting world. Even if He did exist, He was certainly not the God of love and kindness that these religious fanatics rave about. No, He's the God who sits up there and watches. He watches the Germans gas the concentration camp victims. He watches the murders, rapes, and assaults that are perpetuated during each generation. He watches the sick writhing in pain each day. Naaman was a Syrian who was cured of Leprosy by the great prophet Elisha, who a religious associate of mine said performed more miracles in the bible than anyone else except Jesus. He was the only person to be cured of Leprosy. That was very fortunate for Naaman, but what about the hundreds of thousands of Lepers who had to endure their lives of misery during Elisha's lifetime? If I watched a baby slowly creep into the road only to be crushed to death by an automobile, I would feel terrible. I would certainly try to save the baby, provided I was at no risk of personal danger. Instead of helping man in this sewer of a world, God prefers to watch. This all-powerful, all-knowing God prefers to watch. Isn't that exactly what God did when both of my parents were killed in an automobile accident three years ago, May 13? This God of the bible just looks down from heaven and watches the death and suffering. Can you imagine what it must have been like for a Russian prisoner of war to survive a German concentration camp and then return home to find himself in the Russian Gulog? Ask an Armenian about the Turks. Ask a Palestinian about the Israelis. Ask the Russian people about Stalin. Ask the Jews about everyone. They will all tell you about suffering. Where is this God? Is he blind? Is he deaf to man's screams of pain and sorrow?

If thinking about this God isn't enough to get you upset and crazy, then spend a few minutes with a Roman Catholic priest. From the Vatican, we get pronouncements about theological esoterica. Who cares if Mary, the blessed mother of Jesus, never sinned? Who cares about the mystery of the Holy Trinity? I care more about the Holy Inquisition. I care more about the Christian religious persecution of non-Catholics. Is there anything that Hitler did that was not done previously by officials of the Catholic Church or the Catholic kings of Europe? The politics of the Vatican does not differentiate this political institution from the secular governments of Europe. Is there any greater hypocrisy than the Popes and saints preaching the crusades? Whatever happened to loving your neighbor and praying for your enemy? What happened to the guidance of the Holy Spirit?

At least the Catholics have some form of human guidance. Even more pathetic are the various Protestant denominations. Almost any minister may preach what he or she wants to say as long as there is some tangential support offered from the bible. Authority comes from the myriad of interpretations of the bible, and apparently, there was no further religious development since biblical times. Religion developed for thousands of years until Jesus, then God, retired to sit and watch.

Any homosapien could realize that the separation into Roman Catholic, Protestant, and Eastern Orthodox churches results from political and secular conflicts. Could anyone argue that the people of Northern Ireland are killing themselves over theological differences? The destruction of religious unity helped foster this conflict.

If the Christians are so pathetic, what about "God's Chosen people," the Jews? With an outstretched hand and with signs and wonders, God delivered his chosen people out of slavery in Egypt and brought them to the promised land. What a great story! Great for whom? Was it great for the Egyptians, who were also created in God's image? Certainly, they suffered. Life was difficult enough for the average Egyptian without the additional suffering of the ten plagues. Was it great for the Jews? They had to endure four hundred years of slavery, and then the vast majority of those enslaved died in the desert without reaching the promised land. Was it great for the thousands of people in the promised land who were murdered by these hordes of former slaves? I doubt it. If anyone looks at the suffering of the Jews, it is difficult to ascertain any advantage of being chosen by God.

The Moslems were similar to the Jews. After the Arabs were chosen, they immediately set upon a course of war and conquest. Why is it that after God chooses a group of people, they frequently feel compelled to demonstrate their saintliness by attempting to destroy their neighbors?

Across from the coffee shop was Tears Church, Weiskirche. It was a beautiful pastel pilgrim church in a meadow. Its dimensions mirrored the shape of the surrounding meadow. I entered the church, sat down, took off my glasses, and looked at the alter picture of the scourged savior. Jesus was chained and was being whipped. Suddenly I became aware as if a thought or idea entered my mind that there was a God, that He loved me, and that my sins were forgiven. I did not hear a voice. Instead, there was a strange communication that bypassed my brain and went directly to my heart. I arose stunned and dazed but was exceedingly happy. I was so happy. Later I would learn that the alter picture, actually a wooden icon of sorts, was discarded from the Good Friday procession because it was deemed too ugly. A woman recovered it, and later a church was built around the picture when numerous people observed tears flowing from the face of Jesus. Hence the name Tears Church. Except for the alter picture, the interior of the church had rich, beautiful colors.

I leaped onto the bus and noticed for the first time that it was packed with people. October 15, 1982, started like any other day, but it would forever change my life. As we arrived at the castle, I noticed I had forgotten my glasses at the church. Although my vision was markedly impaired, without the glasses, the feeling of utter joy could not be dimmed. I shared a carriage ride to the castle with a couple from Barcelona and a retired American soldier who had been stationed for many years in Karlsruhle, Germany. I actually started a conversation with these three people during the short carriage ride.

Previously such a waste of time would be unthinkable. I asked the couple what they thought was most interesting about Barcelona. They said that the church of the Sacred Family by Antonio Gaudi was most interesting because of its architecture. It was yet to be completed. Money had been collected for about a hundred years, and the church still did not have a roof.

I thoroughly enjoyed the tour of Neuschwanstein Castle. King Ludwig II, considered somewhat of a crazy loner, was obviously not crazy. Anyone who could design and oversee the construction of such a masterpiece had a clear understanding of beauty. Walt Disney copied King Ludwig's castle and built a replica for Disneyland. If ever there was a beautiful castle in a perfect location, this was it.

Still somewhat in a daze, I returned to the boarding house to pick up my backpack. Sticking out of the side of the backpack was a city map of Munich that I had never seen before. It was one of those free maps that tourists obtained at the train station. I asked Mr. Zonna if there were any other backpacks stored in the closet and was told that mine was the only one. No other guest was leaving that Friday. I noticed an "X" on the map and asked the clerk to identify it for me.

"That's easy. That's the Four Seasons Hotel." He answered.

"Perhaps I'll go there for dinner tonight," I said more to myself than to Mr. Zonna.

"Not possible, no, not possible. You need a reservation several days in advance. It is Friday night. The restaurant is small and will be crowded. Besides, no one is permitted there in jeans and running shoes. You must wear a suit and shoes," Mr. Zonna volunteered.

I was going to see for myself. I splurged and took a cab. Next, I gave my backpack to the doorman outside, found the restaurant, and asked the maître d' to be seated.

"Your name, sir," he asked.

"James Paul," I replied.

"Come with me, please, Mr. Paul," he said as he removed the reserved sign from a nearby table. The reserved sign indicated that the table had been reserved for Herr Paul, a party of one. Obviously, I had been invited. Everyone wore expensive clothing. The piano player and all of the waiters wore tuxedoes. From the piano came a melancholy song by Michael Jary, "A Man Like You and Me." I asked the waiter to write down the lyrics in English.

"If a man is rich and powerful,
If a man is a king,
It does not matter.
He is still a slave to his fate.
We are all slaves, whether a king or a beggar,
We are all equal in this world."

The food was delicious, and the service was superb. I left the table to use in the Men's Room. As I sat down to relieve myself, I noticed a unique, pleasant odor instead of the usual foul odor associated with this daily bodily function. Much later, I would understand that I had been invited to this table by the Savior. But for now, I had to pay the bill and catch the train to Vienna. My host must have paid most of the bill because the check was about the same money I spent had I bought bread, fruit, and juice at the train station. As I ran to the train station, I noticed some of the other points marked on the map. I ran beside the Residence of the Wittlesbach royalty from Scandinavia, who had ruled Bavaria for about six hundred years. There was an X over it. I saw the towers of the Frauenkirche, the landmark cathedral church of Our Lady. The church was circled on the map. Circled on the map was a nearby stop for trams 14 and 19. Last was a "J" at the Wittlesbach fountain. I ran to the fountain, hoping to find a word or phrase that started with the letter "J." Instead, next to this magnificent fountain stood a rather small, thin, middle-aged man with a southern accent.

He said, "You must be James. It's about time you arrived. I've been waiting for you. I've been waiting a very long time for you." With that, he turned and walked away, and I ran to catch the train to Vienna.

CHAPTER 2

VIENNA

WHAT WAS HAPPENING? WHY did I feel compelled to leave Munich and go to Vienna? I had a Eurail pass. There were plenty of vacant hotel rooms in Munich in October. Perhaps I should stay in Munich and visit the Residence and the Frauenkirche? Should I take a ride on trams 14 and 19? I felt compelled to go to Vienna that night. I arrived in Vienna the next morning, found an inexpensive room, and fell asleep immediately. I awoke at about six in the evening and was hungry. I found St. Stephen's Café in my travel guidebook. It was not expensive and would be easy to find since it was near St. Stephens Cathedral. It would be easy to find since no building in downtown Vienna was allowed to be taller than the spire of St. Stephens Cathedral. I was tired and would not have to follow a street map.

I walked to the center of the town. Yesterday's events must have been part of my imagination. There is no God, and if God exists, why pick me? Many people cancel reservations at restaurants. Some forget about the reservation and don't show up. What about the unique odor in the Men's Room? Maybe it's some perfume they use in very expensive hotels. Again, the bill was not expensive. They must have added it incorrectly. The man near the fountain with the southern accent could have been one of those people I've seen hundreds of times talking to himself in New York City. Still, there were too many coincidences. Previously, I disliked Germans and Munich about as much as I still disliked the drawn-out Southern accents. Let's face it. If you grew up in New York, you would dislike waiting for a person with a Southern accent to finish speaking. Gomer Pyle would not do well in New York City. The great exception was the man from Mississippi and Florida. The voice of the Brooklyn Dodgers (dem bums) Red Barber. He was educated and articulate. After a few innings, you imagined you were in baseball heaven – springtime, beer, and Jackie Robinson. No, that southern accent in Munich was that extra touch just for me.

St. Stephens Cathedral was in the center of the city. Its northern tower was never completed. However, unlike the Sacred Family Church in Barcelona, St Stephens had a completed roof and was a fully functional cathedral. It was Saturday night, and as I walked looking for St Stephens Café, I heard the church bells. Evidently, I was just in time to go to Mass.

I entered the cathedral, and it was filled to capacity. People were elegantly dressed. The choir was sensational. Later I discovered that this was a special celebration of the fourth anniversary of the election of Pope John Paul II. The Austrian cardinal entered the conclave with material to convince others to elect John Paul II pope, The President of Austria was present, and of course, the Vienna Boys Choir was singing.

I felt good after mass. I was still confused, but it was a pleasant confusion. I was happy, so there was little urgency to examine the details. I opened a glass door to look for St. Stephens Café on the second floor at the address from the guidebook. As I walked into a little hall, I thought I was in the wrong place. There was a dim light on the second floor of the address from the guidebook. No one was in the building. I turned to leave, but the door was locked. I wasn't going to go up to the second floor, since it was too dark and creepy. I was frightened since, being a pulmonary physician and growing up in New York City, most people were familiar with the Coconut Grove nightclub fire in 1921. People were locked in and burned alive. Since then, in most western countries, you could lock the doors when the place was closed, but you were not supposed to lock the doors when the place was open for business. Austria and all western European countries have similar laws. I kept tapping on the glass door, and eventually, a man with dark hair tried to open the door and could not open it. He smiled and left. There was no way out of the hall. I started to shake with fear. Panic set in. I turned around, away from the door, and looked up the stairway to the second floor. There was a bright Christmas tree. Then the tree disappeared. Next, there was a bright Easter candle. The candle disappeared. Finally, there was Jesus. I knew it was Jesus. He looked at me, and I bowed to the floor. I covered my face with my hands and fell to my knees. There was no sound or verbal communication. There was no mental message. With a combination of sweat and tears, I looked up, and the figure was gone. I could barely stand up. Suddenly a lady with blond hair came to the door from the square. As she effortlessly opened the door, she smiled, and I ran into the square. After a few moments, I stopped running. There was no escape from the hall without the help of the lady. I regained my composure. I was safe. I was out of the hall.

The sensation of hunger returned, and I walked into the Lucky Chinese Restaurant. I don't like Chinese food, but this place was perfect. It looked like a real restaurant, well-lighted, with real people serving real customers. That's exactly what I needed at this point who cared about the taste of the food. Let's get back to the real world. Take a few breaths. Relax. Pretend that nothing unusual happened and order some food.

Why was this happening? Am I crazy? Am I caving into all of the stress around me? Wait a minute. What am I thinking about? I'm on vacation, and there is nothing stressful in my life. Work was going well. I wasn't sick. There were no major financial problems. There was no special woman in my life, but there had never been anyone special, and I was never actively looking for one. Sure, my parents died suddenly, but I was over that acute loss, anger, and sorrow. You never recover completely from life's tragedies. Instead, you pick up the pieces and continue as best as you can; but the cracks remain.

After eating, I picked up a piece of paper from the table. Thinking it was the check, I took out my wallet to find my money. However, then the waiter came and placed the bill on a small plate on the table. I opened the piece of paper in my hand and stared at it:

Lucky

Paul

Stephen

Brigitte/Brigid

Four founders

Marcus

Blond at the door

Oct 15	*Oct 16*	*Oct 17*
Germany	*Vienna*	
Four Seasons	*Lucky Chinese*	

No one knew where the piece of paper came from. It wasn't my handwriting. I did not imagine this. There was a real piece of paper. You could touch it, see it and read it. What did it mean? The blond at the door was the person who had just let me out of the hallway. Paul referred me to – Dr. Paul. What about Stephen, Four Founders, Marcus, and Bridgit? Something was going to happen tomorrow October 17, 1982. I'm going to keep this paper; it's the only evidence of my sanity.

CHAPTER 3

OCTOBER 17, 1982

OCTOBER 17, 1982, STARTED without anything unusual. It was a sunny day. I thought a bus tour of the city would give me an overview of the main points of Vienna. I took out my city map to locate the bus tour departure point when I noticed written on the side of the map:

St. Brigit

St. Stephens

There were no other words or markings on the map. I looked at the piece of paper from the restaurant and noticed that it had two spelling mistakes. Now the spelling mistakes have been corrected. Brigid was changed to St Brigit. St. Stephans was changed to St. Stephens. Also, St. Stephens was in the wrong place. God created everything symmetric or with a mirror image. There was also a place for another entry to the right of the last dash.

October 16, 1982, with the two mistakes:

Lucky

Paul

Stephen

Brigitte/Brigide

Four Founders

Oct 15	*Oct 16*	*Oct 17*
Germany	*Vienna*	
Four Seasons	*Lucky Chinese*	
	St Stephens	

October 17 After Corrections:

Lucky

Paul

Stephen

St. Brigit

Four Founders

Marcus

Blond at the door

St Stephens

Oct 15	*Oct 16*	*Oct 17*
Germany	*Vienna*	
Four Seasons	*Lucky Chinese*	

Now it was perfect. My elementary school teachers were correct when they said that spelling counted.

Something unusual did occur on October 17. The message was corrected. There were so many questions. What did the message mean? Who wrote it? Who corrected it? Why were there errors that had to be corrected? Why give me a puzzle to solve instead of just telling me the message?

Instead of trying to answer these questions, I started out on the bus tour.

Vienna was a beautiful city to visit. The monuments from the Hapsburg dynasty were scattered throughout the city. There were beautiful parks, impressive museums, and the river Danube. It reminded me of Munich. As the bus neared St. Stephens Cathedral, I got a chill down my spine. I turned to see the glass door I had been trapped behind. I didn't dare leave the bus to investigate the door and the building. However, from my seat on the bus, I did manage to see a note written on the glass door that was not there the previous night. It was a white sign that covered a large section of the door. It said in German and in English, "Visits Prohibited." Any courage that could be contrived out of curiosity or stupidity immediately vanished. I took a picture of the door and noticed the sign in the developed picture. That's as close to that building as I ever wanted to come.

I went to a bookstore and started to investigate the possible meaning of the message. Paul was either me or the famous St Paul or both of us. There were a few similarities between us: We both hated Christians at one time, were converted instantly, were not married, and received a message. He was told to give the message of the Good News of Jesus, the gospel, to the children of Israel, the kings, and the gentiles of the world. I was given this puzzle to figure out. I hate puzzles. After that, there was no comparison. St. Brigit was a Swedish mystic who was given revelations about the passion (sufferings) and death of Jesus. She was identified with the cross, Friday penance, and the seven sorrows of the blessed virgin Mary. She was not a timid woman of the middle ages and, after a heated argument with the Pope, told him that he was a "murderer of souls." St Stephen was a deacon famous for being the protomartyr of the church. St Paul was present holding the clothing of the men who were stoning St. Stephen to death.

After spending the next few days trying to figure out the meaning of the message, it became obvious that this was beyond my intellect. Either God chose the wrong person, or the meaning of the message would become known in the future. For now, I was finished with the paper.

During the next few days, I started to read the New Testament for the first time. It was very confusing. I had difficulty understanding many of the terms Jesus used: Lamb of God, Sabbath, Passover, demons and evil spirits, healings, and anything related to rural life. So I started to read parts of the Old Testament. Then things became a bit clearer. Apparently, one had to become a Jew or had to at least understand some Jewish thinking before one could begin to understand what Jesus represented and what He was saying.

People have enough difficulty trying to understand the real world that they can touch, see and measure. But there is also a supernatural world that is just as real. Slowly I was being introduced to this world. It is not limited by the concepts of time and space, and man's initial reaction to this world is to disbelieve. One must have the grace, the unmerited gift from God, of faith and courage to get out of the boat during a storm and stand on the water as St. Peter did. One must be taught by signs and prophesies to acknowledge this supernatural world and follow this God-given faith throughout the storm. What is the purpose of the many signs and prophesies if not to assure man of the existence of this supernatural world? How does man submit his free will to the manifestations and demands of this unknowable world? For example, most people would be curious, as Moses was, to investigate why the burning bush was not consumed by the fire. Most of us would react with hesitancy to return to Egypt as Moses was instructed to do. A clear sign is given, the burning bush. But God knows that days later, as you are traveling to Egypt, doubts will arise. Did you imagine all of this? So you remember that there was another sign that you were given at the same time. You were told that your brother would meet you in the desert. Yes, now you can see him; it's your brother Aaron coming to meet you just as predicted. The burning bush was real, and so was the message.

This concept of receiving a sign together with a matching sign or prophecy repeatedly occurs throughout the bible. It appears to be a necessary tool to teach man, to help him differentiate a personal message from God from his own personal thoughts. How is the man to understand the significance of a dream sent from God versus one that is part of his routine nightly dream world? Furthermore, sometimes it becomes necessary to act on the interpretation of divine dream messages immediately without extensive analysis.

Examples of these concepts are provided by the annunciation of the birth of Jesus and the flight to Egypt by the Holy Family. God sent the angel Gabriel to give Mary the message of the incarnation (God would come down from heaven and become man, which is absolutely unbelievable) and the fulfillment of prophecy: A virgin shall give birth to a son, and he will be called Emanuel, which means God is with us. This interpretation of the events of the annunciation is not a detraction of the perfection of the Blessed virgin. Rather it is an interpretation that accounts for her humanity. The annunciation is accompanied by another sign. After Mary is told by the angel that she will call her son Jesus and He will be called the son of God, she receives a further sign:

"Remember your relative Elizabeth. It is said that she cannot have children, but she herself is six months pregnant, even though she is very old. For there is nothing that God cannot do." (Luke 1:36–37).

Soon afterward, Mary visited Elizabeth, who greeted her as "the mother of God." These confirming signs are necessary if human beings are to believe the unbelievable. Joseph's initial reaction to all of this was also perfectly predictable. He was a good man. He would quietly and privately break their engagement so that Mary would not be disgraced publicly. Then an angel appeared to him in a dream and told him that Mary's son was to be named Jesus because he would save his people from their sins. Imagine his amazement when he asked Mary the name she was told by the angel to give to her son. This sign to Joseph was necessary for him to believe in the incarnation and marry Mary. It was also a great learning experience for Joseph. It prepared him for his greatest moment. After the birth of Jesus, he had another dream:

"An angel of the Lord appeared in a dream to Joseph and said, 'Herod will be looking for the child in order to kill him. So get up, take the child and his mother and escape to Egypt. Stay there until I tell you to leave. Joseph got up, took the child and his mother, and left during the night for Egypt, where he stayed until Herod died." (Mathew 2:13-15).

He had to set out immediately. There was no one to consult. There was no time to dissect the true meaning of the dream. No, he knew it was similar to a previous dream, and he acted immediately. We are all indebted to Joseph, the patron saint of the universal church, for saving Jesus.

Well, James Paul, let's get back to the twentieth century and the real world. I am not immaculate. In fact, not a day passes without me committing a variety of sins in thought, word, or deed. I'm certainly no saint. In fact, I've led the opposite of a "saintly life" by whatever definition you might use for that term. I was baptized but never confirmed. Until these recent events, I can't remember attending church except to be present at a wedding out of social obligation.

Perhaps I've been chosen much like St. Paul was on the road to Damascus. He was also traveling. God is the great creator, but He is also the great re-creator. St. Paul persecuted the early church. The Christians in Israel must have hated him for his role in their arrest and subsequent punishment. Throughout his life, the Christian church in Jerusalem was always suspicious of him. Forget about the miracles; they knew him as a murderer. The Jews always hated him from the day he started to preach the gospel. Even today, Jews continue to dislike St. Paul centuries after his death. The Jews are appalled by his view that the Law of God enslaves man and does not justify man (put him right with God). It was St. Paul who urged that following Mosaic law was no longer required. Had he not followed the law when he helped stone St. Stephen? He realized that the law led him to commit murder. The purpose of the God-given law was fulfilled with Jesus. Without the Mosaic law, no one could possibly begin to understand any of the manifestations of who Jesus was and what his death represented. The God-given law was supplemented with centuries of man-made law, and Paul clearly saw that this present first-century law had left him with blood dripping from his hands. There was simply no reason to follow any of the rituals of the Mosaic law as prescribed in his society. Man does not follow a prescribed set of rituals and good acts to achieve heaven. God does not take a man to heaven because it can be earned by doing good deeds. God is never indebted to man. Rather, man the sinner is granted an unmerited gift of faith to begin to appreciate a tiny fraction of God's love. God sent his only son to suffer and die for us sinners. We could never begin to understand the incarnation and the suffering of Jesus for us unless we were given some imperfect analogies from the Old Testament.

God gave us Abraham as an example of His love for us and also as an example of a man of faith. Jews, Christians, and Moslems look to Abraham as the ultimate example of a man of faith. The Moslem is the firstborn son. The Jew is the son of God's promise. The Christian is his adopted son. For many years Abraham was told of the many descendants he would have. He was asked to wait until he and his wife were elderly before they were granted the son of God's promise, Isaac. After Abraham sent his elder son Ishmael, who he had by a slave girl, out of his household, he was left with Isaac. Then God asked Abraham to sacrifice this only son, and Abraham was willing to give up everything for God. It didn't make any sense to Abraham to wait all of these years for Isaac and then kill him., but if that was what he was sure God wanted, he had the faith to do it. God tested Abraham as you would test a friend. But God knows the future, so the test was an example for us. Just as Abraham was pulling back the knife to kill Isaac, he passed the test, and Isaac's place was taken by a ram, a male lamb. Jews read the story of Abraham and Isaac each year on Rosh Hashana. They blow the ram's horn – the shofar – and observe a day of remembrance. God starts his judgment with the horn blowing, and the theme of the prayers for that day is repentance and atonement. Moslems celebrate this special event with the holiday of Eid al Adha, the holiday of sacrifice when they sacrifice lambs as Abraham did. Jesus is the Passover lamb whose blood was placed at the doorposts in Egypt. We are freed from the slavery of the world and delivered from death by His blood. Furthermore, God is personal. He calls each of us by name as a shepherd calls his sheep individually. He seeks us out and actively intervenes in our lives even though we don't realize it. He loves each one of us as if there is no one else to love. After three Jews were thrown into a fire because they refused to worship another God during the Babylonian captivity, the king noticed that there were four men in the fire, not three. The three men who had been thrown into the fire became four men walking in the fire unharmed. The three Jews were saved. The Lord personally enters our fire of suffering to save us. These examples are to teach us that we don't earn heaven by good works. Rather we are given the grace to begin to appreciate God's love for us through our faith. We then respond to this faith in God's love with our good acts. True faith must be accompanied by acts of gratitude. This is what St. Paul taught. Eventually, St. Paul went to the heart of the Gentile world to preach the gospel. The Romans also hated him. They could not crucify St. Paul because he was a Roman citizen, so they executed him with the sword.

Another good example of how God re-creates is the symbol of the cross. In the earthly days of Jesus, everyone understood the meaning of the cross. The Romans had borrowed this form of humiliation, torture, and murder from the Persians. The victim was first beaten and whipped publicly. Then he carried part of his cross to the place of death. He was then undressed and nailed to the cross to hang there until he died a slow, painful death. After death, the body was left for the animals to eat. Could there be a perfect symbol of evil? Only non-citizens could be crucified. Today we no longer witness executions on the cross. The cross is the symbol of God's love for us, of His willingness to personally suffer for us because of His great love for us. We no longer view man's suffering on the cross. The cross now refers to the suffering of Jesus so our sins so can be forgiven.

CHAPTER 4

ROME

I NO LONGER HAD the desire to continue my European trip. Instead, I wanted to go home. I wanted to be in a quiet place, to learn about God's plans, and to reflect upon the meaning of all of these unusual events. But before returning home, I had to visit Rome. I had to visit St. Peter's Cathedral.

St. Peter was probably the only apostle, a witness of Jesus, with whom everyone could identify. If you were uneducated, you could envision this formerly uneducated fisherman from Galilee. If you were formally educated, you might identify with the author of the complicated theological concepts as noted in the Epistles of St. Peter. He was rash and excitable. He would change his opinion at times. He was momentarily undaunted when attempting to walk on water, just like a toddler. He was stubborn and argumentative. How many times did he attempt to correct Jesus? In our ignorance, don't we all have moments of rebelling against kind, well-meaning and intelligent authority? Peter continued to envision the Messiah, the anointed, as the anointed king who would set up an earthly kingdom. The Jews were looking for another Moses. Jews everywhere were praying for liberation from the despicable, heathen Romans. St. Peter rejected the teaching of Jesus that the Messiah was to suffer, be rejected, and die as the lamb of God on the cross. None of the apostles understood this until after the resurrection. But Peter is perhaps best known for his denial of Jesus. Peter is the one who when asked about Jesus said that he did not know him. We could identify with this since all of us deny Jesus daily when we reject His love and use the freedom of our free will to sin.

I always thought that St. Peter received some bad press notices from the story of his denying Jesus. Was he really the apostle who followed Jesus, saw His miracles, and then had a lapse of faith when Jesus, the man, was most in need of a friend? During His last night, Jesus predicted that He would die and that all of the apostles would leave Him:

> "Peter spoke up and said to Jesus, 'I will never leave you, even though all of the rest do.'
>
> Jesus said to Peter, 'I tell you that before the rooster crows tonight, you will say three times that you do not
>
> Know me.'
>
> Peter answered, 'I will never say that, even if I have to die with you.' (Matthew 26:33–35).

At that moment, Peter was ready to die for Jesus. What more can you ask of a man? How much more can he give of himself? After Jesus was arrested, Peter acted on his convictions. He was true to his word; he was ready to die for Jesus. He did not leave Jesus, nor was he concerned about his own safety. In spite of being outnumbered by the Roman soldiers and temple guards, Peter acted.

> "Simon Peter, who had a sword, drew it and struck the High Priest's slave, cutting off his right ear. The name of the slave was Malchus. Jesus said to Peter, 'Put your sword back in its place! Do you think that I will not drink from the cup of suffering which my Father has given me?" (John 18:10–11).

Peter obeyed. He was confused. He wanted Jesus to escape. He was well-intentioned but wrong. He was ignorant, as was everyone else, of the role of Jesus as the lamb of God. Jesus had to suffer and die on the cross to save us. Peter was attempting to disrupt God's plan of salvation. There were many occasions when Jesus escaped arrest because His work was not finished and His time had not come. But this was His time. Just as the destruction of the Temple by the Babylonians and then Romans occurred on the same day, the liberation of God's people by the blood of the lamb – Passover and Good Friday – was also ordained to occur on an identical day in a public well-documented manner. Peter did not understand this. He persevered. He continued to follow Jesus, and this led to his denial. If his main concern was for his own safety, Peter would not have drawn his sword and instead would have fled like the other apostles. Instead, he continued to try to find a way to help Jesus escape. Eventually, he denied Jesus and wept. He was thoroughly confused and dejected.

After his resurrection, Jesus appeared to seven of his disciples in Galilee:

> *'After they had eaten, Jesus said to Simon Peter, 'Simon son of John do you love me more than these others do?'*

> *'Yes, lord,' he answered, 'You know that I love you.'*

> *Jesus said to him, 'Take care of my lambs.' A second time Jesus said to him, 'Simon, son of John, do you love me?' '*

> *Yes, Lord," he answered, 'You know that I love you,'*

> *Jesus said to him, 'Take care of my sheep.' A third time Jesus said, 'Simon son of john, do you love me?' and so he said to him, 'Lord, you know everything; you know that I love you.'*

> *Jesus said to him, 'Take care of my sheep.' (John 21: 15-17).*

Jesus always understands us. He understands our intentions as well as our actions. Peter was given a special place as Prince of the Apostles and leader of the flock.

I purchased my first cross in the Vatican gift shop. After placing it on my neck, I said my last prayers at St. Peters Cathedral and started to return to my hotel room. As I ascended the Spanish Steps near the hotel, I looked up into the clouds and saw the face of Jesus. He had a sad look. His head was straight; that is, He was not looking down as He is so often portrayed on the cross. There was no sound, no voice, and no message. In a flash, the image of His face was gone. Why did He appear in Rome? Why did He wait until I put on the cross? What did the Spanish Steps have to do with anything?

My mind was overwhelmed. There were too many questions and few answers. I was being taught by the ultimate teacher, and my first lesson was patience. Why didn't God just tell me everything He wanted me to know now? At least I was convinced that these supernatural events were real and that I was sane. Then again, how many perfectly adjusted, happy people thought the world was a large sewer and never developed friendships?

CHAPTER 5

HOME

I STOPPED AT THE office the day after I returned home. I was a few days early and thought I might catch up on some paperwork. My senior partner was surprised to see me. He appeared nervous and asked if I might return later in the afternoon. Actually, I was not a full partner in this two-person practice. I still had three months remaining as his associate.

When I returned, I was fired. I was told that the business wasn't going well and that my presence in the office was no longer required. The locks to the doors had been changed during my absence. The patients were to remain in his practice, and I was free to remain at the hospital, although my success would be limited because of the many years he had devoted to the hospital. He said that he had no personal animosity toward me and that this was just an unfortunate business decision. I was stunned. My cash reserves were limited because of my recent trip. Where was this happiness just a few days ago?

As I turned to leave the office, Dr. Reed then told me that I owed him $12,000 in expenses agreed upon according to the terms of the contract I had signed almost two years ago. He then handed me an envelope from his attorney. I had no reply.

I was angry and needed money. I needed a well-paying job immediately. I walked into the hospital medical library to look through some medical journals to find advertisements for physicians. I was flipping the pages trying to figure out why I had not seen this coming. Was I such a poor judge of people to have trusted Dr. Reed? Could there have been something I should have done to avoid this catastrophe? Then I saw an interesting advertisement. It was for a physician to work in the capital of Saudi Arabia, Riyadh. The salary was good. Three weeks later, I signed a one-year contract to begin work the following month. Dr. Reed was correct. There were no other physicians willing to share office space, nor was there anyone willing to alternate night coverage with me. The lease to the may apartment was finished, and Saudi Arabia seemed like a nice quiet place. I had no home or family I was giving up on leaving.

CHAPTER 6

THE KINGDOM OF SAUDI ARABIA WHERE MEN ARE MEN AND THERE ARE NO WOMEN.

SAUDI ARABIA IS THE only country named after a family – Saud. In the eighteenth century, the Saudi family ruled a small area in central Arabia near the present capital. When Mohammed ibn-Saud united the Saudi family with the teachings of the religious reformer Mohammed Abd el-Wahhab a powerful movement was formed. This led to increasing territorial conquests culminating in the capture of the Holy city of Mecca in 1806. The expulsion from Mecca and Medina could not be tolerated by the Turkish Moslem rulers. The Ottoman Turk Sultan sent his viceroy to Egypt, Mohammed Ali, to recapture the Holy lands. The Saudi forces kept up the fight against the Turkish/Egyptian forces for several years. Finally, the Saudi king was executed in front of the Sultan, Saudi soldiers were massacred, and their ears were sent back to the Sultan. The Saudi capital of Dariyah was raised to the ground. Later the Saudi family re-established control over a small part of central Arabia but eventually were exiled to Kuwait, an area ruled by a related tribe.

It was from the exile of Kuwait that the young prince Abd el Aziz al Saud came to surprise the soldiers in Riyadh and begin the conquest of Arabia. The subsequent kings have all been his sons. Members of the royal family occupy all of the important government posts.

My first impression of Saudi Arabia was the incredibly dry heat. It felt like you were sticking your head into an oven. People covered their bodies from the heat. Alcohol and recreational drugs were strictly forbidden. Most conspicuous was the call for prayers several times a day and through the night over the loudspeakers. The commercial activity stopped, and the men kneeled to pray. Islam means submission to God.

As an American schooled in the advantages of democracy over the tyranny of the English kings, the Saudi form of government leaves much to be desired. If one equates good government with each citizen's opportunity to exercise political influence by voting and occupying the political office, then the present form of the Saudi government leaves much to be desired. Trade unions are prohibited. Women are not allowed to drive. However, the Saudi government is very concerned with the welfare of its citizens. The services provided by the government are monumental. How can any Saudi citizen complain? If you want a job, it will be provided for you. If you need money to start a business or fam, the government will let you borrow the money. The government will pay for your education. There is an extremely low crime rate. If you need medical treatment, especially treatments that are very expensive, like surgery, organ transplantation, dialysis for kidney failure, or cancer therapy, it will be provided free of charge.

The tertiary referral center was the Consultants Hospital. Each physician spoke English, and all of the medical charts were in English. Many of the physicians spoke Arabic. All of the resident physicians spoke Arabic. The hospital staff was recruited from all over the non-communist world. In many ways, it was similar to enlisting in the army. Housing was provided for all employees. Permission to travel outside of the kingdom had to be obtained from the hospital.

I was assigned a large apartment that contained every appliance one could imagine. Food was subsidized at the hospital cafeteria.

A large supermarket with American and European products was nearby. The only major problem that could not be overcome was the incredibly hot climate. It could reach 120 degrees F in the shade for a large portion of the year. If you had to walk any distance outside, it was an effort.

The hospital personnel was courteous. The physicians tried to get along because there was no competition for patients. The patients' attitude was the most notable difference in the practice of medicine in the United States. Due to the expense of health care in the United States and because of the malpractice crisis in the United States, there is, at the time, a basic adversarial doctor-patient relationship in the US. Doctors practice defensive medicine. Every patient encounter is the potential for litigation. Patients complain that the prices are too high. In Saudi Arabia, the situation was different. The malpractice crisis does not exist. Medical care and transportation are free. Most of the patients are grateful for their care, but they do complain if, after taking a three-hour trip to the hospital, you can not help them.

Religious freedom does not exist in Saudi Arabia. Islam is the only religion tolerated. There were no Christian religious services, and it was forbidden to bring Christian religious articles into the country. I was fortunate to get my small New Testament bible through customs undetected. Jews are not permitted into the country.

A couple of months passed. I had purchased a small green plant with wide leaves. It was the only thing in the apartment that differentiated my apartment from another, except for my clothes and toiletries. In my loneliness, the plant substituted for human or animal companionship. Each day I would water it but continued to refuse to talk to it. One day I noticed clear liquid drops accumulating on some of the leaves at the edge of the most distal stem. Being totally ignorant about plants and never having purchased one before. I didn't understand if this was a normal phenomenon or a sign of illness. After all, I grew up on the cement of New York City. Their vegetation was divided into three broad categories. If you could walk on it, it was grass. If you could lean on it, it was a tree. If you fell over it, it was a bush. So I placed my plant firmly in the bush category and tried to recall seeing drops of water appearing on some distal parts of bushes I had previously observed. The next morning the drops were gone.

The following day I noticed that the cross I had purchased at the Vatican was no longer in its case on my apartment desk. I was furious. Who could have come into my apartment and stolen my cross? People from security had keys to all of the apartments. A search through my apartment revealed that nothing else was missing.

The next morning the cross was back in its case. Either I was hallucinating, and it never disappeared, or it was returned while I was asleep.

A week later, I was reading from the Letter of Paul to the Galatians:

> *"Let me tell you, my brothers, that the gospel I preach is not of human origin. I did not receive it from any man, nor did any man teach it to me. It was Jesus Christ himself who revealed it to me. You have been told how I used to live when I was devoted to the Jewish religion, how I persecuted without mercy the church of God and did my best to destroy it. I was ahead of most Jews of my age in my practice of the Jewish religion and was much more devoted to the traditions of our ancestors. But God, in his grace, chose me even before I was born and called me to serve Him. And when He decided to reveal His son to me so that I might preach the Good News to the Gentiles, I did not go to anyone for advice, nor did I go to Jerusalem to see those who were apostles before me. Instead, I went at once to Arabia and then returned to Damascus. It was three years later that I went to Jerusalem to obtain information from Peter, and I stayed with him for two weeks. (Galatians 1:11-18).*

I looked up after reading this and noticed that the same drops were accumulating at the distal edge of some of the leaves. Again, I was surprised when I realized that the missing and reappearing cross represented Good Friday and the drops from the plant were similar to tears from the altered picture in Tears Church. I was already in Arabia, and in a few weeks, the Easter celebration would begin in Jerusalem. God had not abandoned me in this desert. The next morning the tears on the plant were gone and never returned.

Saudi Arabia did not recognize the state of Israel. Most maps in the Kingdom depicted the area as Palestine.

Anyone with passport notations revealing a previous visit to Israel would not be admitted to the Kingdom. So making plans to visit Israel would be difficult. The people at the hospital were gracious enough to grant me a one-week leave on relatively short notice. I booked my departure to Cyprus and my return from Cyprus. In Cyprus, I would make arrangements to go to Israel. So in a couple of weeks, I would be landing in Tel Aviv.

CHAPTER 7

JERUSALEM

"Jerusalem, Jerusalem! You kill the prophets; you stone the messengers God has sent you! How many times have I wanted to put my arms around all your people, just as a hen gathers her chicks under her wings, but you would not let me." (Luke 13:34)

WE ARE ALL CALLED to be pilgrims. Indeed our life is one long journey to heaven. Each year a couple of million Moslems make a pilgrimage to Mecca and Medina (Hagg). It is an Islamic requirement that each Moslem with the necessary financial means visit Mecca and Medina once during their lifetime. The Saudi government spends millions of dollars each year to help the pilgrims. Two thousand years ago, Jews were required to visit Jerusalem on certain holidays each year. The early Christians were devoted to the holy places in Israel, and when they were prevented from visiting Jerusalem by the Turkish sultans, the devotion to the Stations of the Cross developed. The Popes encouraged devotion to the sufferings of Jesus by having the churches depict the fourteen points along the Via Dolorosa, the road of suffering that Jesus followed to His death.

Jerusalem was very crowded. The Jews were celebrating Passover at the same time the Christians were celebrating Easter. There was no bread available, only Matzoh, unleavened bread. At noon, on Good Friday, I was part of the crowd that traced the footsteps of Christ along the Via Dolorosa. It started at the place where Jesus was condemned to death by the Roman governor Pontius Pilot and ended at the place where Jesus was placed in the tomb, the church of the Holy Sepulcher. I kept getting the numbers and the order of the stations confused. Good Friday, the day Jesus died and Easter Sunday, the day of His resurrection, are the most important events in the history of the world. Without Jesus' suffering on Good Friday, there would be no victory over death and release from the slavery of sin as proclaimed by the resurrection. Conversely, without Easter Sunday, Good Friday would represent the death of Jesus and a victory for the Evil One. The centerpiece of the Christian religion is the cross and the resurrected Christ. St. Paul considered himself an apostle with the same authority as the apostles who lived with and followed Jesus because he met the resurrected Christ on the road to Damascus.

People were pushing and shoving each other during the Good Friday procession, especially at the end when the last few stations were close together in the Church of the Holy Sepulcher. After the procession, I took a tour of the old city. The tour guide exclaimed the great joy of the Israelis after they captured Jerusalem during the war of 1967. When Jordon controlled this area, Jews could not pray there. They were now able to pray at the Wailing Wall, the western wall, and at the Temple area. This is the most holy place for Jews because it represents a remnant of the Temple, God's house. Actually, the western wall was not part of the Temple; rather, it was the western wall of the outside walls built by the same Herod who had attempted to murder Jesus.

In the narrow walkways of the old city, the sound of increasingly loud shouting could be heard. Suddenly the tour guide directed everyone to dive onto the floor of the adjacent little shop. A group of thirty or forty Moslem men was running through the streets throwing stones. Apparently, a group of Jews had attempted to celebrate Passover at the Temple mount area the night before. This area is now the Dome of the Rock and is the third holiest place for Moslems. It was here that Abraham was about to sacrifice Isaac, and it was from that same spot that Moslems believed that God's last messenger, Mohammed, went to heaven. The Moslem men were now reacting and demonstrating their extreme displeasure over last night's provocation. Fortunately, no one in the tour group was seriously injured. The people of the tour group now had a vivid remembrance of the crude, violent Arabs to bring home.

I have had many discussions with Arabs in Saudi Arabia about the Arab-Israeli conflict. The people of the Middle East live out the intricacies and hardships of this conflict daily. Americans are fortunately far removed.

In the battle of public opinion, it is often stated that the American Jews control the media and present a distorted pro-Israeli view to the duped American public. Many Arabs claim that if the American public were given all of the facts, there would be greater support for the Arab side. Perhaps there is an element of truth to this, but I doubt it. The American public does not care to know the intricacies of this conflict. Opinion polls in the United States repeatedly report the ignorance of the public about current events. Yes, most Americans understand that the Arabs and Israelis don't get along and periodically have a war, but that is the extent of their information and interest in the conflict.

More important than the facts are the pictures of the combatants. With whom would you average American identify? On the Israeli side, there are politicians who speak English with an accent and are dressed as Americans, with the exception that apparently there is a great shortage of ties in Israel. The men might be shown leaving parliament wearing a suit without a tie. With the exception of the missing tie, the image of the Israeli leader is identical to his American counterpart. This is not true of the Arab leader most identified with the Palestinian cause. He also refuses to wear a tie. The single most important element in the battle for the support of the American public is the image of one man–Yasser Arafat. Sure, Americans might identify with Israel because it is a democracy, but most people in America don't care about the form of government of Israel, nor are they listening to the words of their politicians. It is the image that is important. The Jewish lobby is not manipulating anything. Just look at Yasser Arafat!. To the average American, he looks dirty and in need of a shave. He is wearing some rag on his head and is carrying a gun. Is there any other world leader seen carrying a revolver? If they replaced him with a soft-spoken Palestinian university professor, they would immediately gain the support of the American public.

CHAPTER 8

———————————

BACK TO ARABIA

The passport control officials in Israel were familiar with the passport policy of the Kingdom of Saudi Arabia. Many Arabs visit Jerusalem and the Moslem holy land and go back to Saudi Arabia. Thus, upon request when in Israel, the officials will not stamp your passport but instead will issue you a separate card. Upon leaving Israel, the card is returned. Thus, as I entered Saudi Arabia and waited to go through customs, I was confident that there would be no difficulties. The only evidence of my visit to Israel was the tourist slides of Israel that I had purchased that was in my jacket pocket.

I was happy about my trip to Israel. It only lasted a few days, but being there during Easter and Passover was a unique experience. After the plant and cross events, I might have expected the supernatural to re-occur. It did not, but I was not disappointed. I was supposed to go to Israel, so I went there. I was in the right place at the right time. Besides, the supernatural events severely tested my already questionable sanity.

If God wanted to say something to me, why didn't He speak English? If I couldn't understand what He was saying, it was His fault. He's the Creator; I'm just the creature. I remember studying English literature in high school and college. The instructor, a typically frustrated author, would lead a discussion about what the famous author of the classic we were reading was trying to say. Then we would be tested for what appeared to be high-grade reading comprehension, similar to elementary school. This made no sense to me. I could appreciate learning about the devices authors employed with the stream of consciousness and dialogue so that the reader felt that he was in the action of the novel and not just flipping pages. But reading comprehension for the author's audience seemed to be something the author should use to gauge his ability to get his message across. Didn't the instructor realize that these authors were dead and could not benefit from constructive criticism?

The Saudi immigration official looked through my passport and stamped my entrance visa. Then I went to the familiar counter to open my suitcase and have them go through my belongings. Suddenly another official squeezed my jacket pocket and realized that I was hiding something. I was instructed to go to a separate room with my suitcase. Three soldiers went through my belongings. Sweat started ripping down my face, not from the heat but from the thought of being incarcerated in a Saudi prison. The soldiers looked through some of the slides. It was obvious that they were tourist slides purchased in Israel. I made a feeble attempt to explain to them that the Allah they believed in was God, the Father. In doing so, I denied the role of Jesus, whose crucifixion and resurrection I had just celebrated. Slowly I repacked my suitcase. I was too nervous to close it correctly, and the soldiers intervened to close it for me. I waited as a verbal report was given to one of the officers. The officer spoke English. The verdict was guilty. They knew that I had been to Israel, was hiding the slides, and was attempting to deceive them by going to Cyprus.

Then the officer turned to me and said, "We check pictures and slides because foreigners bring in pornography to sell to our children and young adults. Remember, if you have been to Israel, you are not permitted to enter Saudi Arabia. As a person of the book (Mohammed referred to Jews and Christians as people of the book bible), I hope you had a successful Hagg (Arabic word for pilgrimage). You are free to leave." He held out his hand to shake hands with me.

I was ashamed of myself. Again it was revealed that I was a weak, frightened human being with perhaps an over-active imagination.

> *"I assure you that whoever declares publicly that he belongs to me, the Son of Man, will also do the same for him before the angels of God. But whoever rejects me publicly, the Son of Man will also reject him before the angels of God. Anyone who says a word against the Son of Man can be forgiven, but whoever says evil things against the Holy Spirit will not be forgiven." (Luke 12:8-10).*

I had just denied Jesus in a feeble expression of misguided fear. Again, was I weak and crazy, or was I being led by the Holy Spirit? Perhaps I was all of the above. No, that couldn't be possible. There are many examples of weak, ordinary men who were chosen by God and strengthened by His spirit. Never had God chosen someone who was insane. King David, when he was fleeing for his life, faked insanity at one time. He was a young man anointed by God via the prophet Samuel. David was led by the spirit of God and defeated the Philistine giant Goliath. Then he was hunted down by a jealous king Saul. Things became so bizarre that even though David spared Saul's life, he again had to flee to save his own life. He left Israel to hide amongst the Philistines. In fact, just prior to Saul's death at the hands of the Philistines, David offered his benefactor his help in battle. They did not trust him to fight his own people and declined his offer. Things could get confusing even if you were chosen by God.

Back at the hospital, I welcomed the routine. Periodically I would think about the future and returning to the United States. I missed the change of seasons. I missed my own culture, the local newspapers, and professional sports. Here, work was the only distraction. I was in an air-conditioned hospital and apartment, but it was still the desert. How people survived in the desert decades ago prior to electricity was beyond my imagination.

I began to pray. It was a simple conversation with God. There was no one else to talk to in this desert. I didn't know any formal prayers. I had heard of the Lord's prayer and remembered that it started with "Our father who art in heaven…." I never learned the rest of the words. I simply did not understand the purpose of prayer.

> *"Your father already knows what you need before you ask Him."* (Matthew 6:8).

If He knew what I needed and knew the future, perhaps He would provide for me. Maybe He was a great Santa Claus waiting for requests. No, there had to be more to prayer than selfishly asking for gifts. I needed a lot of help learning how to pray.

> *"This, then, is how you should pray: Our Father in heaven, May your holy name be honored, May your Kingdom come. May your will be done on earth as it is in heaven. Give us today the food we need. Forgive us the wrongs we have done, as we forgive the wrongs others have done to us. Do not bring us to hard testing, but keep us safe from the Evil One."* (Mathew 6:9-13).

This is the end of the twentieth century. Few people now believe in the existence of demons, Satanic possession, or the association between illness and sin. Yet, there it was. Jesus suggested that we pray for safety from the Evil One. As a physician, I usually welcome dealing with a sick patient from a religious family. You would try your best to help the patient, but the family realized that you were only a man. To those whose god is science, when a family member is ill, they look to the physician as a king of science. They will not easily accept an unfortunate outcome without mixing their sense of loss with some blame for the king. When the patient expires, the religious family is comforted by the fact that God's will was done and there is an afterlife. It gets confusing. If I try hard to save a sick patient, and then he dies, was I fighting the will of God? What is the will of God?

The Lord's prayer teaches us to call God our father. No father wants to see his child suffer. So from where does the evil and suffering of the world come? His will being done on God's will is not always done. Perhaps ultimately, His will is achieved when we get to heaven. But what about His will being done on earth as the prayer suggests? Obviously, there is an Evil One. He is the Prince of Darkness and the Ruler of the World. It is from this source and from man's free will to sin that all evil and disease originates. It is not so simple that when each person sins, he receives his share of the suffering. The world we live in is not fair.

As a physician, I don't view the sick as a sinful individual. If you are exposed to an infectious disease, most likely, you will get sick. There are natural laws that are followed. So where is the relationship between sin and disease? There is a collective sinfulness. There is a corporate sinfulness of man. Perhaps ultimately, His will is achieved when we get to heaven. If man had not devoted so much time and so many resources to attempt to destroy his neighbor, perhaps he could have more quickly developed the cures and prevention of illness that we call modern medicine thousands of years ago.

The famous story of Adam and Eve can be interpreted as an allegory about sin. The deception of the Evil One disguised as a serpent was a necessary ingredient. This came first! This active plan of the Evil One occurred prior to anything that Eve said or did. There followed an intellectual acknowledgment that the instruction of the serpent to eat the apple was directly opposite to the commands of God. Then there was the free will choice of Eve. There was also a free will choice of Adam. I don't think that Eve physically shoved the apple down Adam's throat. Shame followed; then came hiding and the denial of fault.

Christ died to deliver us from the slavery of sin, from the slavery of the Evil One. God's marvelous creation has been enslaved by the Evil One. Jesus prayed for his disciples.

> "...now I am coming to you, and I say these things in the world so that they may have my joy in their hearts in all its fullness. I gave them your message, and the world hated them because they do not belong to the world, just as I do not belong in the world. I do not ask you to take them out of the world, but I do ask you to keep them safe from the Evil One." (John 17:13-15).

Hence, there is another supernatural power operating in the world. There is open warfare between the forces of good and evil. There is a supernatural, superhuman war between Jesus and the

Evil One. The outcome of the war was already decided when Jesus achieved victory for us by dying on the cross. However, although the victory has been achieved, the war is not over. We each have our own battles to fight. When someone is sick and in pain, it is not the will of God, our loving Father. It is the will of the Evil One. When natural tragedies occur, it is not the will of God; rather, it is the will of the Evil One. All wars are the result of the will of the Evil One and the sin of man. How can a man fight this supernatural evil? It is only through prayer and the gifts of grace. The Evil One may be a ruler of the world, but Jesus has told us not to worry because He has conquered the world.

CHAPTER 9

NEW JERSEY

I HAD ACCUMULATED ENOUGH vacation time to return to the United States. During my vacation, I interviewed at a number of pharmaceutical companies in New Jersey. Running clinical trials would be interesting. There was no night call, and weekends were free. A year in the desert was enough.

I settled into the job and discovered St. Lukes Catholic Church had a mass that started at seven o'clock each day. I could attend mass and then get to work at the official 8:30 AM starting time. The church was built in 1921 and had beautiful stained glass windows. The priest, Father Sullivan, started each service with the Angelus prayer. This is a prayer recounting how the angel of the Lord appeared to Mary to announce the birth of Jesus, Mary's acceptance to be the Mother of God, and the incarnation. It is punctuated by three Hail Mary prayers which begin with the words of the angel, "Hail Mary full of grace, the Lord is with you." Many Catholic churches have bells that ring to announce mass and call the people to worship. The pattern of the church bells follows the Angelus. It starts with three sets of three bells for each of the three Hail Mary prayers and then continues with a set of regular bells, perhaps thirty or forty, representing the rest of the prayer. Mary is calling us to her Son.

One day during the summer of 1984, an idea came to my mind. It was strange. The idea was two numbers: 2 and 22.9. This idea was totally unrelated to my previous thoughts. It happened shortly after I asked Father Sullivan about the developments in the church. I remember he asked me if, on the day of Pentecost, when Christians celebrate the birth of the church because the Holy Spirit descended upon the apostles, would St. Peter have eaten with the Pope? I told him that it sounded like a trick question, so the answer was probably no, but I didn't know the reason for the answer. He told me that I was correct because, at that time, Peter would not eat with gentiles. He wanted to make the point that church development through the guidance of the Holy Spirit continues; it continues to this day.

Several days later, I realized that 2 and 22.9 referred to two readings from the Acts of the Apostles. Chapter 2 describes the day of Pentecost: 22.9 is the line from St. Paul's description of his conversion "The men with me saw the light, but did not hear the voice of the one who was speaking to me." (Acts 22.9). At that time, he was called Saul. Saul was the one who hated the church, and after his conversion, his name was changed to Paul.

"As I was traveling and coming near Damascus, about midday, a bright light from the sky flashed suddenly around me. I fell to the ground and heard a voice saying to me, 'Saul, Saul! Why do you persecute me?'

Who are you, Lord? I asked.

I am Jesus of Nazareth, whom you persecute," He said. "The men with me saw the light but did not hear the voice of the one speaking to me."

I asked, 'what shall I do, Lord?'

And the Lord said to me, 'Get up and go into Damascus, and there you will be told everything that God has determined for you to do.'

I was blind because of the bright light, so my companions took me by the hand and led me to Damascus. (Acts 22:6-11).

The men near St. Paul could understand that something had happened to him because he was blind, but they could not hear

God's personal message to St. Paul. It reminded me of October 15, 1982, when I left my glasses at Tears Church.

The change of name from Saul to Paul was significant. Many times in the bible, a person's name is changed. Examples include Jacob to Israel, Abram to Abraham, and Simon to Peter. James and John were called the "Sons of Thunder." Each of these people was important in God's plans.

CHAPTER 10

THE DREAM AND THE LIGHT

ONE EVENING DURING THE summer in 1985, I was awakened from sleep by a dream. It was the number 17. This was very unusual because I never recalled having dreams. The last dream I could remember was when I was six years old. I came running out of my bedroom in the middle of the night to play with a boy who used to live next door (Joey). It seemed so real. In the dream, we were playing in the kitchen. For the rest of my life, I could never remember any dreams. I learned as a medical student that psychotic patients might repress the memory of their dreams. Everyone else dreams each night and remembers a small portion of their dreams. The content of the dream was unusual. It was 17, which had no significance to me.

Several weeks later, I started to have difficulty sleeping. I would awaken each night around 2 AM – 2:30 AM and stay up for a few hours. I tried eating, reading, and watching television. I set the clock earlier and altered several routines, but nothing helped. Psychiatric patients frequently have trouble sleeping through the night despite the sedatives that are frequently prescribed for them.

One night around 3 AM, I was watching a news/interview show. The moderator had a southern accent which was very unusual for television in New Jersey. I kept thinking that if only the moderator could take lessons to get rid of his accent, he would have a great future because he was very good. The only light in the room came from the television. Suddenly three of the four lights in the room came on. They stayed on for ten to fifteen seconds and then turned off. No one was in the apartment except me. I was wide awake; this wasn't a dream. Lights just don't turn on by themselves unless there is a timer. There was no timer for these lights. I started to again try to convince myself that I was sane. What did the three lights mean? What did the number 17 from the recent dream mean? Why did it happen when the newscaster with the southern accent was on television? I had no clue.

With the lack of dreams punctuated by the unusual dream of 17, insomnia, and finally seeing lights go on, I again started to question my sanity. I didn't believe a psychiatrist could help me, nor was I convinced that I was in dire need of psychiatric treatment. I also realized that my non-existent female social life would not progress until the issue of my sanity was resolved. I wasn't insane enough to seek help; perhaps that was a sign of my illness. On the other hand, I could not mention these supernatural events to anyone without appearing crazy. What sane, desirable female would want to have anything to do with me? Furthermore, I wouldn't want a relationship with any female who thought I was crazy. What kind of women would that be? It reminded myself of the Groucho Marx line, "I wouldn't want to join a club that wouldn't want me as a member." He said this in reference to a private club that did not allow Jews.

I was thinking about this social predicament while driving to work on September 6, 1985, when I had the misfortune of stopping at a red light. It was just not the right time to stop, but I didn't realize that. The next thing I remember was waking up in the intensive care unit. A truck had smashed into my car from behind as I was waiting at the red light. It pushed me into the intersection, where my car was hit on the side by a car whose driver had unfortunately not stopped for the green light in his direction. I promised the driver of the car, who was in bed next to me that I would not stop at the red light if he stopped at the green light. I explained to him that the accident could have been prevented if I had driven through the red light and he had stopped at the green light. He was unconscious while I was explaining all of this, but his nurse, who was perfectly awake, seemed to agree with me. I recovered in a couple of days. The other driver recovered also. The CAT scan of my brain was normal.

CHAPTER 11

EASTER, 1986

THE THREE LIGHTS CONTINUED to puzzle me. It did not represent three days, three weeks, or three months. Finally, I knew it stood for three years. How I realized this was another mystery. It was now several weeks before Easter, and soon it would be three years since I visited Jerusalem on Easter. I wanted to prepare for this special day. I went to confession for the first time. Although I had confirmed the previous November, I had yet to receive the sacrament of reconciliation. I went to St. Thomas the Apostle Church because I was embarrassed to go to St. Mary near my house or to St. Luke near my work. St. Thomas was a scientist of sorts. He had some bad press reviews and was often referred to as a "Doubting Thomas." He doubted the other apostles when they told him that after Jesus died, they had seen Him walk through closed doors and heard Him speak. Would you believe this collection of misfits without proof?

> Thomas said to them, *"Unless I see the scars of the nails in his hands and put my finger on those scars and my hand in his side, I will not believe." (John 20:25).*

Who could blame him? Just days ago, Jesus was crucified, and a spear was pushed into His side to make certain that He was dead.

Now He is supposed to be alive, walking through doors or walls and conversing with the other apostles. They ate and slept together, following Jesus. Perhaps that is why he didn't believe these fishermen, tax collectors, and zealots. It was one thing to believe Jesus but quite another to have to believe what these people were telling him. Thomas wanted proof, not their word.

A week later, the disciples were together again indoors, and Thomas was with them. The doors were locked, but Jesus came and stood among them and said, "Peace be with you." Then he said to Thomas, "Put your finger here and look at my hands; then reach out your hand and put it in my side. Stop your doubting and believe."

The only requirement was to believe in Jesus. It was a requirement to be an apostle and to go to heaven. Intelligence, charm, and all of the worldly attributes were not required. Again, Jesus returned for His stray sheep. Thomas responded to Jesus by believing in His resurrection and divinity when he said, "My lord and my God."

After I introduced myself to the priest, there was a long silence. He was waiting for me to proceed, but I didn't know what to say. Finally, he asked how long it had been since my last confession. I told him that this was the first time I was here. Then he asked me to list my sins in a general way to save me some embarrassment. Finally, as a representative of the church, the body of Christ, he absolved me of my sins. For penance, I was to say some prayers

A few weeks later, after Mass on Easter Sunday, I was leaving St. Lukes church near work when Father Sullivan told me to wait. He had a gift for me. I was surprised. People don't exchange gifts on Easter except perhaps some chocolates and Easter bunnies. I had no gift for Father Sullivan. He gave me a medal with the name St. James the Greater on it and a small plague with some words written by St. Paul:

"Love is patient and kind; it is not jealous or conceited or proud; love is not ill-mannered or selfish or irritable; love does not keep a record of wrongs; love is not happy with evil, but is happy with the truth. Love never gives up, and its faith, hope, and patience never fail. Love is eternal." (1 Corinthians 13:4–8).

I thanked him for the gifts. Nothing else that was even remotely unusual occurred that day. I kept trying to make sense of the three lights, 17, and the gifts from Father Sullivan. There were two apostles named James; St. James the Greater was the brother of St. John. I thought I would read the Letter of James from the bible. Various people have been suggested as the author of that epistle. Since St. James, the Greater, was the first apostle to die, and he died in 44 AD, many people believe that it was some other James in a position of authority who wrote the letter. Many scholars believe that the Letter of James was one of the earliest writings that has now been accepted as the New Testament. I was intrigued by the ending of the letter:

"Is anyone among you in trouble? He should pray. Is anyone happy? He should sing praises. Is there anyone who is sick? He should send for the church elders, who will pray for him and rub olive oil on him in the name of the Lord. This prayer made in faith will heal the sick person; the Lord will restore him to health, and the sins he has committed will be forgiven. So then, confess your sins to one another and pray for one another so that you will be healed. The prayer of a good person has a powerful effect. Elijah was the same kind of person as we are. He prayed earnestly that there would be no rain, and no rain fell on the land for three and a half years. Once again, he prayed, and the sky poured out its rain, and the earth produced its crops.

My brothers, if one of you wanders away from the truth and another one brings him back again, remember this: whoever turns a sinner back from the wrong way will save that sinner's soul from death and bring about the forgiveness of many sins." (James 5:13-20).

If you counted Easter Sunday as day one, then April 15, 1986 would be day 17. April 15, 1986 was also exactly three and a half years from October 15, 1982 when I was converted in Tears Church. So before retiring to bed on April 15, I read these lines from the letter of James and prayed. Then I fell asleep. At exactly 2 AM on April 16, 1985 I awoke from sleep with another dream. It was two couplets of number: 7,11 and 4,23. Then I went back to sleep.

CHAPTER 12

─────

THE ROSARY

ONE DAY AFTER MASS at St. Mary's Church, the church near my apartment that I attended on weekends, I noticed a small group of people saying a series of prayers with prayer beads in their hands. The only thing I knew about the rosary was that it was a series of prayers associated with the Blessed Virgin Mary. There was no mention of the rosary in the bible. During my days in the desert, when I was reading the bible every day, I noticed very little about Mary. There was one story in the bible about Mary that was difficult for me to understand:

> *"When the wine had given out, Jesus' mother said to him, 'They are out of wine.'*
>
> *'You must tell me what to do,' Jesus replied.*
>
> *'My time has not come.'*
>
> *Jesus' mother then told the servants, 'Do whatever he tells you.'*
>
> *Jesus said to the servants, 'Fill these jars with water.'*
>
> *They filled them to the brim, and then he told them, 'Now draw some water out and take it to the man in charge of the Feast.'*

They took him the water which had now been turned into wine."
(John 2: 3-5, 7-9).

This was the first miracle that Jesus performed. It was the start of His public ministry. Through the intercession of Mary, who always instructs us to do whatever Jesus tells us, the grace of God was revealed at that time. Many non-Catholic Christians view the asking of Mary or a saint to intercede for us as the beginning of a cycle toward polytheism. They do not understand that asking for a saint's intercession is not praying to the saint. It is asking someone who is near God to pray for us. God has always used prophets inspired by His will as an intermediary to the people. Also, there are many times when these special people intervene with God on behalf of the people. Abraham bargained with God not to destroy Sodom and Gomorra if ten good men could be found. Even today, Jews do not start public prayers without a quorum of ten men. Moses intervened with God not to destroy His people.

When we ask Mary to intercede for us, we are not praying to Mary to perform a miracle. Only God performs miracles. Instead, we are asking her to pray for us. All prayers go to God, including Mary's prayer for us. Didn't St. James tell us to pray for each other so that our sins may be forgiven? Now we are asking the Mother of God, the Queen of Heaven and Earth, to pray for us. Many Protestants will ask a friend, minister, or family member to pray for the sick family member. So why not ask Mary to pray for us? Mary and the communion of saints do not perform miracles, but they are alive, close to God, and will add their prayers for us.

The rosary is a prayer asking Mary to pray for us. It is composed of decades of ten Hail Mary prayers. Each Hail Mary ends with the following phrase: "Holy Mary, Mother of God, pray for us sinners now and at the hour of our death." Each decade starts with the Our Father prayer, then ten Hail Mary prayers and is followed by the "Glory be to the Father, the Son, and the Holy Spirit as it was in the beginning, is now, and ever shall be, world without end." Each series is recited while one of the "mysteries" of the life of Jesus and Mary is contemplated. There are five joyful mysteries: the annunciation, the visitation (Mary visits Elizabeth), the birth of Jesus, the presentation of Jesus in the temple, and the finding of Jesus in the temple.

There are five sorrowful mysteries: the agony of Jesus in the garden of Gethsemane, the scourging of Jesus, the crown of thorns, Jesus carrying the cross, and the crucifixion. There are five Glorious Mysteries: the resurrection, the ascension of Jesus to heaven, the coming of the Holy Spirit, the assumption of Mary to heaven, and the coronation of Mary as Queen of Heaven and Earth. Before beginning the mysteries, the apostle's creed, three Hail Mary prayers, and one Glory be to the Father are said. Usually, one of the series of five mysteries is said each day. Some people pray all fifteen decades each day. The series of prayer beads is also called the rosary.

Mary wants us to pray the rosary each day. She wants us to ask for her powerful intercessions so that we will receive more graces from God. It is these graces that help us fight withthe Evil One.

CHAPTER 13

7,11 AND 4,23 AND THE TRIP TO ST. ANNE'S CATHEDRAL

WHAT DID THE FOUR numbers from the dream at two AM on April 16 represent? The 7 went the 11. The 4 went with the 23. Also, the order within each couplet was specific. That is, it was 7,11, not 11,7. Also, it was 4,23 and not 23,4. Finally, the 7,11 couplet was before the 4,23 couplet. I thought about these numbers for a couple of days and still could not find their meaning. At first, I thought that they represented dates and that something was supposed to happen on April 23 and July 11, but April 23 passed without anything unusual occurring. Then on May 2, the seventeenth day, if you counted April 16 as day one, I knew that the 7,11, and 4,23 went with the 14 and 19 on the map of Munich on October 15, 1982. It was a series of six numbers, and anyone from the United States will tell you that a series of six numbers like these represent the winning lottery numbers. I was going to win the lottery somewhere! For the first time in my life, I started purchasing lottery tickets. The gospel reading that day for May 2, 1986 was the following:

> *"I do not call you servants any longer because a servant does not know what the master is doing. Instead, I call you friends because I have*

told you everything that I heard from my father. You did not choose me; I chose you and appointed you to go and bear much fruit, the kind of fruit that endures. And so the father will give you whatever you ask of him in my name. This is what I command you: love one another." (John 15: 12-17).

I became interested in a bus trip to St. Anne of Beaupre Cathedral near Quebec City in Canada. St. Anne was the mother of Mary. This church devoted to St. Anne has been a place associated with miracles for three hundred years. Many people have left their crutches at the church after a miraculous healing. We arrived on July 25 just in time for the candlelight prayer procession of the stations of the cross. Afterward, I heard the priest sing the following to the tune of the song: "Edelweiss." Good St. Anne, Good St. Anne, bless your pilgrims forever...

I felt that this was a special song similar to the one played by the piano player in Munich (A Man Like you and Me). Edelweiss is the national flower of Austria, and any of the Von Trapp family from the Sound of Music will tell you the music is associated with Austria.

The next day I discovered that July 25 was the feast day for St. James, the Greater. I was in the gift shop looking for a book about the lives of saints. Suddenly I turned white. I started to tremble. On the page for July 23 used to describe St. Bridgit was a picture of a blond. The face of St. Bridgit from the book was identical to the face of the blond who opened the door for me to get out of the hall on October 16, 1982 in Vienna. Furthermore, St. Bridgit was on the piece of paper, and the spelling was corrected the next day, on October 17, 1982. Things were starting to fit into place.

The church service at St. Anne de Beaupre (beautiful meadow) was magnificent. Thousands of pilgrims attended mass on July 26, the Feast day for St. Anne. Many sick people came hoping to be healed. Services were held in English and French. It reminded me of another pilgrim church – Tears church, which was in a beautiful meadow.

CHAPTER 14

BACK IN NEW JERSEY

THE PENNSYLVANIA – NEW Jersey area contains manylarge multinational pharmaceutical companies. Developing a drug that is getting approved for the American market is a large investment of time and money. It takes about ten years of development and millions of dollars before there is any financial return. Usually, a prospective drug product is identified in the laboratory and tested for effectiveness and safety in laboratory animals. This is phase one. Then phase two, small pilot studies in normal human beings – not patients, are done to demonstrate the drug effect and the dose needed to obtain that effect – dose-ranging studies. In phase three, large clinical trials with hundreds of patients from several centers are reported to the Federal Drug Administration – FDA. If the large phase III studies prove safety and efficacy, then the FDA approves the drug for the market.

Most multinational companies submit clinical data and animal laboratory data to the FDA from foreign countries, where it is less expensive to get the work done. That is why American clinical trials are usually the last in the series of trials for the world development of a drug product. It is also easier to obtain approval to market a drug in Europe than in the United States. When a new drug is first marketed in the United States, it has usually been on the market in several European countries for a few years. This is good because it protects the American public from being exposed to a potentially toxic product. However, it also deprives the American public of a safe and effective drug product for a few years while it is available in Europe.

When the manufacturer is given the approval to market the drug product, it is in effect, granted a patent to sell the drug at the highest price the market can bear. Until the patent expires and the generic competition starts, each drug product is a monopoly business. The manufacturer can protect the drug product monopoly by obtaining patents on the drug substance, method of manufacture, clinical indications for the use of the drug product, the dosage used for treatment, method of the drug delivery (oral, time release oral, parenteral) and even the packaging of the drug product. When a pharmaceutical company losses patent protection on a major product of its major market, sales revenue drops dramatically.

Finally, there are phase four studies that follow approval. All reports of any problem with safety or efficacy are forwarded to the FDA.

CHAPTER 15

CHANGING JOBS AND THE COMPUTER

A COUPLE OF MONTHS later, I was approached to work at a different pharmaceutical company in the same area.

I was offered more money and a greater opportunity for advancement. It was close enough to my other job so that I wouldn't have to alter my weekday routine of going to St. Luke's church. After giving proper notice at my present job, I would be starting 1988 at the new job.

One weekday, as I was driving to work after leaving St. Jukes church, I decided to get a lottery ticket. Just before I was about to get out of the car, a strange feeling told me to look up and open the window on the driver's side. I heard three church bells; that is, there was the sound of church bells ringing three times. Again it was after mass at about 7:30 – 7:45 AM. I bought my now famous losing lottery ticket – 7,11,4, 23,14, 19 – thinking this was the day! Of course, none of those numbers were chosen. God must have a pretty sick sense of humor to be leading me on like this.

The only other unusual thing was directly related to my work. It was Friday, November 13, 1987, and I was told that there were some errors in the data of a clinical trial and that I had to recalculate the statistics. The investigators or their nurses measure the various parameters during the clinical trial and enter the values in the case report forms. This data is then entered into the computer manually at the pharmaceutical company. The computer program helps make charts for the data display and does the calculations for the statistical comparisons.

I was using a non-parametric statistical evaluation for one of the parameters in the three treatment groups. This may sound complicated, but it is really very simple. The data did not follow a normal curve distribution. So one way to analyze the data was to give each value a number based on its relative order compared to all of the other values. The data would then be ranked. Then it could be evaluated after each of the ranking values was assigned to the three treatment groups from which it came. There were three of four errors noted when taking the data from the case reports forms and entering them into the computer. I had never seen the case report forms. I just worked with the data that had already been entered. I corrected the errors and had the computer recalculate the statistics. When this happens, the final results of statistical significance are usually unchanged. That is, the change of a few data points out of a couple of hundred data points does not change the overall statistical significance between the treatment groups. What does change is the number of the statistic that you calculate, the P value. It will change in value by a few thousandths.

I looked at the P value and was momentarily stunned because it was the same number to the fourth decimal place. It had not been altered even though the numbers that the calculation was based upon were different. Then I realized that this was a rank order test. The numbers themselves were not part of the calculations. Obviously, the errors negated themselves, and the relative ranking in each group remained the same. Since the rankings within each group remained the same, the calculation of the P value would come to the same number. However, for some reason, I was curious, and I looked at the numbers again. I could not believe what I saw. The errors did not balance out in the ranking at all. I showed this to several people, and each said that I must have looked through the case report forms previously and corrected the data previously. I just forgot how efficient I had been earlier. I thanked them for their opinion and left to get some fresh air. If I were given this problem to solve, I would have come up with the same conclusion they did. However, I knew that I didn't correct the data from the case report forms. I never saw them. Besides, just a few moments ago, I did correct the data in the computer. The only conclusion was that the computer had acted in a strange way that was not following its program. This is not possible. Then again, I had seen the impossible so many times that I was ready to accept it.

I looked at the data for several days. I wasn't a computer genius, but I didn't have to be one to realize that what happened was not possible. The computer simply did its own thing as if it was infected with a computer virus. I ran a safety check, and there was no virus on the computer.

CHAPTER 16

THE NEW JOB – JANUARY 1988

THE WORK AT THE new job was identical to the work at the old job. Just what I needed, stability. The only difference was that I had to go to the company doctor for a complete history and physical examination. This was the standard procedure for new employees. I felt healthy and thought that this was a waste of time. The physician agreed with me. I had no symptoms, and my exam was normal, but they still had to take some blood tests and a urine test.

Two weeks later, the doctor handed me my chart and told me that all of the tests were normal. I looked at the chart, and all of my values were in fact, normal. I mentioned that there was an error in my height. My height was listed as six feet and two and a quarter inches. I told him that my height had been six feet and one inch for the past fifteen years. People in their thirties do not grow an inch taller. He said that I must be mistaken since his nurse was very efficient. So I took off my shoes again, and they measured my height together. Didn't they have something better to do? They were right! I had grown an inch since last year.

I walked out of the office, thinking to myself that this must be a new syndrome. Increased height and body hair at the age of thirty-eight. By now, I was starting to realize that the impossible was indeed possible. I didn't understand any of this. Who would care if I was six feet and two inches tall instead of six feet and one inch tall? I'm not a professional athlete. If God wanted me to be six feet two inches tall, why didn't He have me grow the normal way? Who could care how much hair I had on my chest?

CHAPTER 17

OUR LADY OF FATIMA

ON MAY 13, 1918, Mary appeared to three shepherd children, Lucia, Jacinta, and Francesco, near a small village in Portugal. Initially, only the girls could see Mary. Then Mary told them that Francesco should pray the rosary, and then he, too, would be able to see her. Minutes later, rosary in hand, Francesco was able to see and hear Mary. Mary asked the children to come to the same place at the same time (noon) on the thirteenth day of each month until October. She told them to pray the rosary each day. She did not mention who she was that day, but she did say that she was from heaven. She told them that saying the rosary each day would bring peace to the world, a world in the midst of World War I.

The next month on June 13, 1917, at noon, she appeared again. The children were told to say the following prayer after each decade: "Oh my Jesus, forgive us our sins. Save us from the fires of hell. Lead all souls to heaven, especially those most in need of your mercy." Lucia, the oldest child, was told to learn to read and write. Jacinta and Francesco were to go to heaven soon. Lucia was to remain on earth to spread the devotion to the Immaculate Heart of Mary. Mary's Immaculate Heart is a symbol of her motherly love for us, her earthly children. On July 13, 1917, the children were shown Hell and given secrets. They were told that God was greatly offended by man and that man should repent. If man did not repent, a war worse than the present World War I would start during the reign of Pope Pius XI. Russia is to be consecrated to the Immaculate Heart of Mary by this Pope in union with all of the bishops. If not, Russia will spread evil, destroy nations and persecute the church. Eventually, Russia will be consecrated, but it will be late. In October, a great miracle would be performed at Fatima so that all would believe the three children.

On August 13, 1917, the children could not meet Mary because, on their way to the noon meeting, they were kidnapped by the government. People who came to the appointed spot at noon reported strange phenomenon of light and sound. On August 15, 1917, the children were released from prison. Mary appeared to the children on August 19, 1917, at a different location and at a different time (4 PM). Again the children were told there would be a miracle on October 13, although they were not told what the miracle would be. People were leaving money at the place the children were meeting Mary. When the children mentioned the money, Mary told them that it would be for the Feast of the Rosary on October 7.

On September 13, 1917, the children again met Mary at noon at the usual location. At noon on October 13, 1917, Mary informed the children who she was. She was no longer the lady from heaven butMary, the mother of God. At noon there was the miracle of the sun. People were able to look at the bright sun directly without shading their eyes. The sun danced and moved around in the sky.

The children were able to see first the Holy Family representing the joyful mysteries of the rosary, then Our Lady of Sorrows and Jesus the redeemer representing the sorrowful mysteries, and then Our Lady of Carmel representing the glorious mysteries. This was similar to what I had seen on October 16, 1982. First, there was the Christmas tree (joyous mysteries), then there was the Easter candle (sorrowful mysteries), and finally, the dazzling white Jesus (glorious mysteries). In a few years, Jacinta and Francesco died. Lucia became a nun. As of 1990, she was still alive. If one considers the German invasion of Austria in 1938 as the beginning of World War II, then it did start when Pius XI was the pope. Russia has indeed persecuted the church.

I always thought that the kidnapping of the children on August 13, 1917, to prevent them from meeting Mary, showed the power of the Evil One. The Queen of Heaven and the children had agreed to meet at noon on August 13, 1917. Yet, the meeting never took place. The Evil One is always working to oppose God's plans. On October 13, 1917, there was a man dressed as a priest who told people to leave since Mary was not coming.

Mary also told the children that she would return a seventh time. Many people believed. Many years later, on May 13, 1981, Pope John Paul II was shot in front of the Vatican. The following May 13, the Pope visited Fatima with Lucia. He thanked Mary for her intercession.

The Moslems do not believe that Jesus was the Son of God. They do believe that He was a prophet from God, similar to the Old Testament prophets. While the Moslems dismiss the reports of the appearance of Mary, they do have a tender spot for Fatima. Mohammed had no surviving sons, but he did have a daughter named Fatima. Perhaps that was why she chose this remote place to appear. The Jews, Christians, and Moslems are all her children.

CHAPTER 18

———⌇⫘⌇———

FEBRUARY, 1988

On February 8, 1988, I was in St. Luke's church. Mass had just been completed. I went to the bathroom, and as I returned inside the church, I sensed a message to "look up" as I did outside the place where I purchased the lottery ticket. I heard the same quality of church bells. The bells were loud, and there was a relatively long interval between them. The interval between the bells was similar to when the priest presented the body and blood of Jesus. The altar boy rings a bell one time with each. I heard two rings of the bell separated by a long pause. I felt surprised, as I always did when these events occurred, but I was not stunned or shaken. These unusual events seemed normal now. I was convinced that I was being taught and led by the Holy Spirit to do something. I still had no idea what I was supposed to do. The associate pastor and other people in the church did not hear the bells.

A couple of weeks later, I went to buy the lottery tickets. I thought I would buy three tickets that day, each with the same number, 7,11,4,23,14,19. I wrote the same numbers on the three tickets and handed them to the man behind the counter, and gave him three dollars. He handed me back the three cards I had just filled out and four lottery tickets! He told me that I owed him a dollar.

So I gave the man another dollar and waited expectantly for the lottery drawing that night. Again I lost my money as other numbers were selected.

A few days later, I was again at St. Luke's church. In many ways, I felt that St. Luke's church was my home. I was saying the rosary in front of the icon when suddenly I heard a noise coming from a wooden box in the wall from the right side. When I turned my head to the left, the noise from the box decreased in volume. I turned my head back to the right, and the noise increased in volume. It lasted about ten seconds. I finished saying the rosary and then asked Father Sullivan about the box. He opened it with a key and showed me that it contained three holy oils. The next day I brought him a small vial and asked if he could give me some oil from the middle vial. As he poured some of the oil into my vial, he told me that this oil was consecrated by the bishop for anointing the sick.

He didn't mention that it was to be used only by priests and that he should not have given it to me.

A few days later, someone at work mentioned that his mother had a hard mass in her neck, and after seeing two Ear, Nose, and Throat physicians, she was scheduled for surgery the next week. He knew that I went to church and asked me to pray for his mother. They were frightened and suspected of cancer. The surgeon also suspected cancer because he had asked my friend's mother to sign consent for a very radical face and neck surgery to be done if the intraoperative biopsy came back malignant. I told him that I would pray for his mother and invited myself to see her.

The patient was almost sixty years old. She had taken a course of antibiotics about four weeks ago to see if the mass would change. It was still rock hard, not movable, and was getting bigger. It was not painful. The only time I ever felt a lesion like that was when it was malignant. The mass was about three inches in diameter and had been present for about five months. I told her that I would pray for her. I could not guarantee any miracles. I was just a man, a sinner like everyone else. I'm just a blind beggar. Only God heals. Then I said the fifteen decades of the rosary and read from the letter of James andthe letter of Paul. I said the stations of the cross and then anointed her forehead with the sign of the cross using the holy oil. It took almost an hour. Then I felt the mass. It was still there; it had not changed. I left and returned home.

I tried my best. I prayed. Obviously, God does not work for me. He doesn't grant all of my requests. If He did, I would forget that I was the creature. I'd probably feel responsible for running the world if I was God's boss. The world is already in enough of a mess without me running it. Still, I had to admit that I was disappointed. Perhaps it was wishful thinking, but I wanted the lady to get better. She seemed like a very nice person; so was my friend. I should have listened to my own advice a little more carefully when I said that I couldn't guarantee anything.

The next week I got a call from the woman when she was in the hospital. She said that she thought that the mass was getting softer and smaller. She was scheduled for surgery that afternoon and asked if I could come and visit her now. She had been afraid to touch it recently. I felt the mass. There was no doubt about it. It was softer, and it was now freely movable. Perhaps it was a bit smaller. She asked me what she should do. I told her to tell her surgeon what she thought. I wasn't going to tell her to refuse consent for the surgery and to discharge herself by singing out against medical advice. I wasn't her doctor, and I couldn't cancel her surgery. Besides, every miracle I had read about in the bible was instantaneous. At the medical commission at Lourdes, each healing is evaluated to see if the healing was miraculous or consistent with the course of the disease or treatment. The healing had to be instantaneous for it to be considered miraculous. Still, the mass was softer and now was no longer matted down to the adjacent structure in her neck. She chose to have the surgery that afternoon. The intraoperative biopsy was benign and the lesion was removed without extensive surgery. She would have a small scar on her neck, and the next day, she was happy that it was over.

A couple of days later, I read the following:

"They came to Bethsaida, where some people brought a blind man to Jesus and begged Him to touch him.

Jesus took the blind man by the hand and led him out of the village. After spitting on the man's eyes,

Jesus placed His hands on him and asked him,

'Can you see anything?'

The man looked up and said, 'Yes, I can see people, but they look like trees walking around.'

Jesus again placed His hands on the man's eyes. This time the man looked intently; his eyesight returned,

And he saw everything clearly." (Mathew 8:22-25).

Obviously, I had a lot more to learn. I wasn't ready. Healing can occur in stages. Perhaps if I had more knowledge and faith, the lady would have been spared surgery. The mass really did change; it was going away.

CHAPTER 19

MARCH 1988

On March 8, 1988, I went to St. Luke's church. After mass was over, I went to the Men's Room. Then I returned to the church and started to pray. I noticed the sound of bells again. They were distant. They did not sound like the bells I had heard during the Stations of the Cross, nor was the quality of the sound similar to the two bells I heard from above the church on February 8, 1988. These bells were different. There were seven bells in patterns – 2, 2, 2, 1, and they were coming from a stained glass picture of the Lost Son. There was no church in that direction. Again, the bells were heard at the usual time after morning mass at St. Luke's church on a weekday, and there were no other church bells ringing.

I started to think about the pattern of the bells – 2, 2, 2, 1. As I prayed for insight into this puzzle, I started to think that it was a pattern of signs. The first two bells represented the match of the two days when I heard the bells at the seventh station. The quality of the bells on those two days was identical (July 9, 1987, and July 10, 1987). The next two bells were for the bells I heard in the parking lot of St. Mary's church. They were not identical, but they were heard at the exact same place (July 11, 1987, and 27 days prior to daylight savings time in 1987). The next two bells were for the identical-sounding church bells after getting the impulse to "look up."

They were the loud bells of St. Luke's church. The last of the bells were for March 8, 1988. I looked at the picture of the Lost Son and started to read from the Bible:

"Jesus went on to say, 'There was once a man who had two sons. The younger one said to him, 'Father, give me my share of the property now.' So the man divided his property between his two sons. After a few days, the younger son sold his part of the property and left home with the money. He went to a country far away, where he wasted his money in reckless living. He spent everything he had. Then a severe famine spread over the country, and he was left without a thing. So he went to work for one of the citizens of that country, who sent him out to his farm to take care of the pigs. He wished he could fill himself with the bean pods that the pigs ate, but no one gave him anything to eat. At last, he came to his senses and said, 'All of my father's hired workers have more than enough to eat, and here I am about to starve!' I will get up and go to my father and say, 'Father, I have sinned against God and against you. I am no longer fit to be called your son; treat me as one of your hired workers' So he got up and started back to his father.

He was still a long way from home when his father saw him; his heart was filled with pity, and he ran, threw his arms around his son, and kissed him. Father, the son said, 'I have sinned against God and against you. I am no longer fit to be called your son.' But the father called to his servants, 'Hurry! He said. 'Bring the best robe and put it on him. Put a ring on his finger and shoes on his feet. Then go and get the prize calf and kill it, and let us celebrate with a feast! For this son of mine who was dead, but now he is alive; he was lost, and now he has been found.'

And so the feast began.

In the meantime, the older son was out in the field. On his way back, when he came close to the house, he heard the music and dancing. So he called one of the servants and asked him, 'What's going on?'

'Your brother has come back home," the servant answered, 'and your father had killed the prize calf because he got him back safe and sound.' The older brother was so angry that he would not go in the house, so his father came out and begged him to come in. But he spoke back to his father, 'Look, all these years, I have worked for you as a slave, and I never disobeyed your orders. What have you given me?

Not even a goat for me to have a feast with my friends! But this son of yours wasted all of your property on prostitutes, and when he comes back home, you kill the prize calf for him.'

'My son, the father answered, 'You are always here with me, and everything I have is yours. But we had to celebrate and be happy because your brother was dead, but now he is alive; he was lost, but now he has been found.' (Luke 15:11-32).

Again, I looked at the stained glass window picture. The father and the lost son were embracing. The servants were bringing the robe and the sandals. The ring was missing! The third gift was the ring, and it was not in the picture. I looked at the other windows in the church and examined them carefully. There was one other window with a mistake. The birth of Jesus, the third joyful mystery of the rosary, was depicted in one of the other windows. There was Mary, Joseph, and Jesus. The infant was in the manger. All were surrounded by a few animals in the barn. Bowing before the Holy Family were the three wise men from the East. They presented their gifts of gold, frankincense, and myrrh to the Holy Family. This was the mistake. The three visitors did not meet Jesus on the day He was born. They came later when the Holy Family was in a house. I remembered the two mistakes on the piece of paper on October 15, 1982, St. Bridget and St. Stephens. That was corrected. I tried to understand. Perhaps the trial would be over when the door opened (St. Bridget, the blond at the door). Then I, the lost son, would become an instrument of divine healing.

CHAPTER 20

PROBLEMS AT WORK – APRIL 1988

IT WAS MID-APRIL. I had been working at my new job for three and a half months. Everything seemed to be going fine. I came to work one morning and found a memo on my desk. The company would be moving to another part of the country. Most people, especially those with seniority, would be offered positions. There would be a gradual cutback in personnel. The move was to take place in six months. When I asked my boss about the memo, he said that both of us had about six months of employment. My old company had started severe personnel cutbacks also. Well, I still had a few months of work left.

I missed seeing patients, but I didn't miss the night call or the work on the weekends. I started to enquire about work in ambulatory clinics. I worked a couple of shifts in some of the ones near my apartment and didn't care for this work, but I had very little choice. It was difficult to get a job in the pharmaceutical industry because of all of the layoffs, and I didn't want to commit to a private practice position, so I was stuck doing this kind of work until things opened up in the pharmaceutical industry. On April 22, the first set of layoffs was announced. Everyone in my section was fired, including my boss. Many of the people were crying. The development of our project was discontinued. I went home and went to bed.

At two AM, I was awakened by my doorbell. Every other day my doorbell rings with the seven chimes with the pattern 2, 2, 2, 1. Now I sat up and counted twenty-seven bells in a regular pattern. I was tired. I didn't want to figure out puzzles at two AM, so I went back after checking that no one was at the door.

The next morning I tried the doorbell and it had the usual 2, 2, 2, 1 pattern. Perhaps I was being reassured that I still had a job with God. But couldn't He do it at another time besides 2 AM? Again the doorbell rang. The pattern was the usual 2, 2, 2, 1. There was only one of these series of seven rings. I opened the door, and no one was there. A few minutes later, there were five series of the seven bells. Again no one was at the door. A few minutes later there were two series of seven bells, but they were spaced much further apart. It was similar to the body and blood bells of February 8. Then I realized that today was April 23 of the 4,23 couplet!

I sensed that the one set and the five sets represented today, day one, and four days from now, day five, respectively. I looked up the readings for today, Saturday, and Wednesday. When I saw the readings, I remembered the 2 and 22.9 readings of Peter at Pentecost and the conversion of Paul. Now here they were again in a different form.

The readings for Saturday, April 23, 1988 included this from the Acts of the Apostles:

> Peter traveled everywhere, and on one occasion, he went to visit God's people who lived in Lydda. There he met a man named Aeneas, who was paralyzed and had not been able to get out of bed for eight years.

> 'Aeneas,' Peter said to him, "Jesus Christ makes you well. Get up and make your bed."

> Then he arose immediately. (Acts 9:31-42).

Four days later, on Wednesday, April 27, 1988, the reading described St. Paul and St. Barnabas being set apart by the Holy Spirit to begin their great missionary work. St. Paul was now ready to start his work after waiting so many years. St. Paul was called on the road to Damascus. Then he went to Arabia. Three years after his conversion, he went to Jerusalem to meet Peter. Then he was sent back home to Tarsus, where he probably waited some more years. He waited until St. Barnabas came to Tarsus on his own initiative. St. Barnabas thought that St. Paul might be able to help him with his work in Antioch. It was from Antioch, Syria that St. Paul and St. Barnabas set out to start their missionary work. St. Paul was converted in Syria and would set out to do his work from Syria. He waited in the desert, was abandoned by the church of Jerusalem, who continued to mistrust him because of his past and then waited in Tarsus. By the time he set sail, he was ready to begin his mission to the gentiles. St. Paul had to be prepared because the world would attempt to stop his preaching. Besides being imprisoned several times, he had to endure many other trials:

"Five times I was given the thirty-nine lashes by the Jews; three times I was whipped by the Romans, and once I was stoned. I have been in three separate shipwrecks, and once I spent twenty-four hours in the water.

(2 Corinthians 11:24-25).

Back in the twentieth century, this Christian was having difficulty finding employment. Perhaps I was spending too much time and energy thinking about bells, readings, and saints. Perhaps I was buying lottery tickets and escaping life in some religious hallucination. My first calling was to avoid starvation. It's a good thing that I didn't have a family to support. Since October 1982, my financial status has deteriorated profoundly.

CHAPTER 21

SUFFERING

Jesus told us that in order to be His disciple, we must pick up our cross each day and follow Him. This is the only way. Every saint, every prophet, has suffered. God does not give you the cross. He does not like to see His children suffer. Yes, there are some exceptions. The children at Fatima were asked if they would like to suffer for others. One of the visionaries in Yugoslavia has accepted a tremendous amount of suffering to help others. That is not the usual pattern. More commonly, God chooses an individual to do His will. Then the Evil One comes with the cross of suffering attempting to stop God's plan. The man then has the choice of either carrying his cross and fulfilling his mission to do God's will or giving up and walking away from the cross and God's will. St. Peter told us that the Evil One does not sleep and is always on the prowl to snare us. Just prior to His arrest, Jesus prayed that His cup of suffering, His passion, cross, and death, would be removed. He was a man, a complete man. What normal man would want to be tortured, publicly humiliated, and murdered? But He was also the Son of God, the Lamb of God, and God Himself as a member of the Holy Trinity. He asked his father if there was any other way to God's will of redeeming man might be accomplished. Then God answered His prayers by saying,

"No! There was no other way to save man." Jesus took up His cross and obeyed His father to the death.

"They came to a place called Gethsemane, and Jesus said to His disciples, 'Sit here while I pray.' He took Peter, James, and John with him. Distress and anguish came over him, and he said to them,

'The sorrow in my heart is so great that it almost crushes me. Stay here and keep watch.'

He went a little further on, threw himself on the ground, and prayed that if possible, he might not have to go through that time of suffering.

'Father, he prayed, 'My father! All things are possible with you. Take this cup of suffering away from me.

Yet not what I want, but what you want.' (Mark 14:32-36).

Jesus revolutionized the concept of suffering. The sick person, the one who suffered greatly, was thought to have personally sinned to such a degree that he brought God's curse upon himself. It followed that the poor, sick, and suffering were the living damned, and these people were frequently tortured even further by the remainder of the self-righteous population. Jesus argued that the sick were indeed suffering because of the corporate sin of the world and the Evil One. Involuntary suffering is from the Evil One. Thus, the kingdom of God was promised to the poor and suffering. Those suffering should be treated with compassion, not derision. With his many healings, Jesus was proclaiming His power to release us from the Evil One. The Evil one will make us suffer but don't lose heart because Jesus has conquered the world.

Conversely, the wealthy, healthy person was thought to be blessed by God because without such a blessing, how could man become successful. It followed that the rich and healthy were assured of heaven unless they lost God's blessing. After Job lost his wealth, his children and his health, his three self-righteous "friends" came to comfort hm by telling him that his sins were the cause of all of this. Jesus stunned the world of His time when He said:

"How hard it is for rich people to enter the kingdom of God! It is much harder for a rich person to enter the Kingdom of God than for a camel to go through the eye of a needle."

The people who heard him asked, 'Who then can be saved?' Jesus answered, 'What is impossible for man is possible for God.' (Luke 18:24-27).

Jesus was confusing everyone with His claim that the rich, who everyone called blessed, was not assured of a place in heaven. He went even further to say that it was almost impossible for the rich to enter heaven. Have the rich become the new group of the living damned in this topsy-turvy world of Jesus? No, the rich were not damned any more than the poor were to be damned previously. Right now, I wouldn't mind joining the rich group. However, the rich do have obstacles to overcome. We all enter heaven by the grace of God. The rich and powerful must overcome their sense of pride. They have less of a tendency to feel dependent on God than the poor.

A series of events brought me to increasing poverty and debt. Every time I went for an interview for a good position with a pharmaceutical company or for a private practice opportunity (I had reconsidered private practice because of my poverty), the result was rejection. I interviewed about twenty times in various parts of the country and was rejected each time. Perhaps I was insane, and this came across during the interview. Should I get an attorney because I was being discriminated against? Sure, I was insane, but I could do the work. After months of rejection and waiting, I finally took a job with the Department of Corrections at the prison near St. Lukes Church.

CHAPTER 22

THE DEPARTMENT OF CORRECTIONS

PRISON MEDICINE IS THE ultimate confrontation and the most odd form of the doctor-patient relationship. There is never a doctor-patient relationship; rather, there is a doctor-patient-security staff relationship. The person in charge is concerned mainly with security, the safety of the public in the surrounding area, and internal security within the prison. The patient is there to see the physician to obtain a personal benefit, cure for his sickness, or improvement in some aspect of prison life. If the patient is in solitary confinement, he may demand medical attention to relieve his boredom. If a prisoner wants to change his bed to a lower bunk, he will tell you about his back pain. If there is an advantage to being on a special diet, he will bring his list of gastrointestinal complaints. If he decides to explore the world of medical technology to relieve his boredom, he will demand medical tests and specialty treatment.

The prisoner is guaranteed access to medical care. He is not free to seek alternate care, so you are stuck with each other. You can never refuse to see the patient, no matter how abusive he may be, because the minute you limit his access to medical care, you will immediately be sued for a real or imagined illness with the help of the ever-present free legal advocate.

The prison was a maximum security facility for prisoners who had been convicted of the worst crimes. I never wanted to know the patient's crime or his term of incarceration. I tried to limit our conversation to the "medical problem" at hand, real or imagined. The prisoners were verbally abusive. Although frequently left alone with the patient in the examining room, the door was always left open, so I could call for help if needed.

My medical co-workers and the security personnel were, at times, even more odd than the prisoners. The prisoners were forced to be there. I was there because I was forced to be there since I couldn't get a better position. I promised myself that if I ever was imprisoned, I would attempt to get into solitary confinement and isolate myself as much as possible from both the prisoners and the staff.

The drug problem inside the prison mirrored the drug problem throughout the United States. Frequently I would be asked to evaluate a prisoner who the staff thought was "under the influence." The drug problem was rampant despite the security staff. Politicians and civic leaders cry out in despair about the frustrations in the battle over drugs. But in prison, it became crystal clear that the drug business could not exist without the encouragement and help of the government. DRUGS ARE A BUSINESS. Someone produces a product. Someone markets the product. There is an element of government regulation of the product. Finally, someone consumes the product. As in any business, the bottom line is profit. How is it possible for all of these consumers to know how to get the product at the same time those in security (police on the street) can't find the drugs?

Perhaps it is a little more obvious in prison, but it is the same outside of the prison. The government must be involved in the drug business for it to exist. Government officials know where the raw materials are grown, where the manufacturing process occurs, points of heavy transportation, local distribution points, and the people who reap the profits. Millions of consumers have access to the product. Finally, the profits must be laundered through large financial organizations.

The true frustration in the battle over drugs comes from the realization that the American public needs and wants drugs. There is a fundamental demand. It is an ugly realization. We want drugs, we buy drugs, and then we complain about the drug problem. Is it the same old story of failing to look at ourselves as the cause of our problems? It is always the other guy who is at fault. Perhaps that is exactly what I was doing when I described my financial problems. Is it really me? Am I insane? Are the religious arguments about the suffering caused by the Evil One part of my psychosis? Maybe I am psychotic and hallucinating about bells, lights, and numbers. Were all of the saints who suffered paranoid when they prayed for safety from the Evil One? I was getting very confused.

CHAPTER 23

MORE SIGNS

I CAME HOME FROM work after picking up my check from payroll. I changed my clothes and started to look for my check and banking forms to make a deposit. I found the banking forms but could not find my check. Because I was behind in paying the rent for my apartment, I had been very careful about putting the pay check in my wallet. I remembered folding the check, placing it in a compartment of my wallet, putting my wallet in the deep part of my front pocket, and placing my rosary above the wallet in my pocket. I was alone when I went through security, and I wasn't near anyone from the time I received my check until I arrived home. There was nothing wrong with my memory. After all, I had just been to the payroll office within the hour. I dreaded having to ask the payroll office to stop payment on the check because it would take a couple of weeks to get another check issued.

The next morning while I was getting dressed to go to St. Lukes church and then to work, I opened my closet to get something. As I opened the closet door, I noticed something falling from the air. I picked it up and recognized it as yesterday's missing check. This was another supernatural sign.

While working at the prison, I continued to ask agencies to find me another job. Every couple of weeks, I would go for another job interview. I became friendly with one of the employment agents, and after one particularly disappointing rejection for a private practice position, I asked him if he could inquire further as to why I had been rejected. A few days later, he called me and explained that with every interview and employment opportunity, a call would be made to the chairman of medicine at the last hospital that I was associated with when I practiced with Dr. Reed. I interrupted him to say that I had left the hospital with my staff privileges intact and that the chairman of medicine liked me. Then came the bomb! Dr. Reed had been the new Chairman of Medicine for the past year. While his letter to my prospective employer was innocuous enough concerning the status of my privileges and good record, after the interview, the prospective employer would call the hospital. It was at this time that Dr. Reed implied that my character and competence left much to be desired. I called Dr. Reed, and he hung up on me. What did I ever do to him? The pharmaceutical companies would also call him. There was no way out of this problem.

During the summer of 1988, I had two dreams. In one of the dreams, I was driving home from work, saying that I was late. I was supposed to be there at noon, but instead, I arrived at 6:30 PM. I understood that I was late, but late for what? The other dream was similar. It was pouring. I got out of my car to make a telephone call to some unknown person, telling them that I was late.

On Friday, July 15, 1988, as I was driving to work, I was saying the rosary. When I got up to the second sorrowful mystery, the scourging of Jesus, the idea came to me of three couplets of numbers 7,11, 4,23, and 14,19. These three couplets matched the three names on the piece of paper in October 1982. The 7,11 date of the thirty-four Angelus bells at St. Mary's Church with Marcus, the thirty-fourth pope whose feast day was October 7, the feast of the Holy rosary. Thus, this set identified a prayer for Mary's intercession, the rosary. Next was 4,23, the date of the four series of doorbells at my house. The readings were about Peter and Paul. This correlated with the four founders on the piece of paper. In the Mass, next came the four readings from the bible on Sundays. Peter and Paul were obviously two of the four founders of the church. The first reading I was given was from the Letter of James. His brother St. John must be the fourth founder. I needed reading for St. John. I also needed a gospel reading. Furthermore, there were two healing stories for the reading with Peter, so I needed two gospel readings for everything to match. John 14 and John 19 seemed to fit perfectly. In John, chapter 14, Jesus tells His disciples that He will die and promises then the Holy spirit. In John 19, Jesus is whipped (scourged), condemned, crucified, and buried. After the reading, the mass continues with the consecration by the priest of the Body and Blood of Jesus. I'm not ordained to do this. The next couplet, 14,19, also matches with St. Bridgit from the paper. It stands for the sacrifice of Jesus. The stations of the cross fit this, and the cross is identified with St. Bridgit. St. Bridgit was devoted to His passion. Finally, the priest distributes the Host, sacrament of communion. Again, I'm not a priest, nor was I meant to be a priest if I pray in this fashion. However, I was given the oil from the middle bottle.

I was to anoint the sick with the oil at this time. There it was. It all fit so beautifully. There was such a combination of prophesy, coincidence, and supernatural signs that the message could not be missed. Also, if I yielded to my periodic feelings of doubt and questionable sanity, I had to admit that I would not be intelligent enough to make up such a story. The origin of this message was supernatural, hopefully divine.

Another interpretation of some of the other signs pointed to the same result. A look at April 23 was a mini sign within a sign. The regular bells at two AM were again the intervention of Mary. There were the regular twenty-seven bells in the parking lot of St. Mary's church and the change of the clock one hour that day. The clock time became correct at two AM, daylight savings time. Next was the series of bells 1, 5 with readings about Peter and Paul, the founders. Then there were the two series of bells with an interval between them that was longer than usual. It matched the body and blood bells of St. Lukes church.

Also, there was the seven bells pattern of 2, 2, 2, 1. That fit also. There were two series of bells at St. Mary's Church. There were the bells that started at the seventh station and at St. Stephens Episcopal. This correlated with Stephen from the paper. Next came the two episodes of the sensation to look up that fit the body and blood.

It fits the stations of the cross. Finally, there was the last of the seven bells from the Lost Son picture depicting the father embracing his lost son and giving him gifts. Here is the gift of the oil.

There was a lovely picture that fit so beautifully. However, it could be all wrong. There were other pieces of the puzzle that had yet to occur. There was "lucky" on the piece of paper. Perhaps this had to be lottery numbers. There was the blond, St. Bridget, the lady of the passion and cross, who let me out of the hallway. There was the disappearing and reappearing pay check. Furthermore, no one has ever been called to pray for healing as their sole mission. The healing, like any other miracle, is a means to accomplish God's plan. So, where is this going?

CHAPTER 24

MORE PROBLEMS AT WORK

ON OF THE DEPUTY superintendents of the Department of Corrections, Mr. Hall came to visit. He asked to see me. After some small talk, he explained the reason for his visit.

"I've been receiving complaints about you from most of the nurses each day. Also, a couple of patients complained about you. Prison medicine is not for everyone, you know. It's best that you resign. You know there are a lot of people here with low moral character, and I can smell a setup. Yeh, you can smell a set up about to take place," warned Mr. Hall.

"I've done nothing wrong. This is outrageous," I protested.

"Look, you're pretty stupid. I'm doing you a favor, and you're too stupid to realize it. There is too much involved. If you don't resign, charts will be altered, and charges of professional misconduct will be filed against you. It's for wanting your own good. Don't you want to leave now, or would you like to be an inmate?" he threatened.

"Can't there be any other way out of this? I really need this job now," I pleaded.

"This is too big for them to worry about one person. You are going to be taken out of here one way or another. I don't think you are listening to me. Hey, you are going to be fine. In a couple of days, a bright guy like you will catch on somewhere. Look, your paycheck has already been prepared and is waiting for you in payroll. You can pick it up now. You will find something extra as a going away present," he promised.

As I dragged myself over to payroll, I wondered how I got myself into this mess. Mr. Hall told me that I was pretty stupid and bright. I guess it took a rare combination of talent to get into such a mess. He was right. There was something extra. There was my regular pro-rated paycheck in the envelope, together with five hundred dollars. They didn't have to do that. Perhaps they were really doing me a favor of sorts.

A few weeks later, I realized that someone did like me and was doing me a favor. Apparently, there was too much competition in the drug business. One of the businesses was eliminated or at least suffered a severe set back in its operations. It started with some small fighting in the area where the prisoners lined up each morning to get their prescription medications. Then the fighting spread to the yard. Extra medical help was brought in from another prison. The physician they hired to replace me called in sick that day. Mr. Hall was correct. If I were a smart businessman, I wouldn't trust someone like me to look the other way. I want someone with a family to threaten me.

CHAPTER 25

OCTOBER AND NOVEMBER, 1988

ON OCTOBER 6, 1988, I noticed that the kitchen clock battery needed to be replaced because the clock was stopping periodically and was falling behind. I didn't have money to waste on a new battery. The holes in my underwear were getting larger. I was losing muscle mass from eating a protein-deficient diet and getting fatter from eating all of the cheap carbohydrates.

The next day the clock stopped at 6:30. Yes, it was the Feast of the Holy Rosary, and there was 6:30 from my dream from a few months ago. I had also been told of my upcoming poverty. My paycheck would be taken away to fall from the sky the next day. Well, not exactly. I was working in ambulatory clinics. It was not a full-time job, just a few ten-hour shifts periodically. I could get my old job back in Arabia, but I wanted to be able to go to church, and I hated the desert heat.

On Saturday, October 15, 1988, I was in my apartment. I had the three small lambs on in the room when suddenly, one of the lamps went out. I went into the kitchen and looked at the broken clock; it was stopped at 9:58. Then I returned to the room with the lamps, and I saw the lamp go back on by itself. October 15 was already very special to me. It was six years ago that I walked into Tears Church as a tourist.

The sequence of walking into the kitchen to see the broken clock and returning to the room with the lamps was almost automatic. I knew what I was doing but had no idea why I went to look at the broken clock. 9:58 is the time that the lottery numbers were selected. I was still spending two dollars a week on the lottery. I didn't have enough money to renew my automobile insurance, but I still hoped to win the lottery. I wasn't a compulsive gambler, but I just had to buy my ticket. I didn't gamble on anything else. On October 15, 1988, the lottery numbers were again not the numbers I had selected.

The next week on October 22, 1988, I lost again at the lottery. The winning numbers were 2,5,15,16,17,27. These numbers meant something to me. Again, God speaks to us in our own language. My language might seem odd to someone else, but this must be the way my brain works. 2,5, 27 refer to the doorbells on April 23, 1988. The 27 was the regular bell at 2 AM. 15,16, 17 were on the piece of paper and referred to October 1982. I would finally begin whatever work I was supposed to do.

October 22 was a special day for Pope John Paul II. He was elected on October 16 and was installed as Pope on October 22. Pope John Paul II was connected was somehow connected with all of this. I hoped to figure this out before I died and before he was shot again.

On November 5, 1988, I was again hoping for my numbers. It was Saturday, and I was ready to collect my money on Monday. There were three other numbers on my ticket – 414. That night I lost again. I was starving on the cheapest food I could buy, and I went to bed hungry and dejected. Suddenly I was awakened from sleep, sat up, and had a thought in my mind. It was "next week," and I looked at my clock to see that it was 4:14 AM. It was not a dream; I was wide awake. Now I was too happy and excited to go back to bed.

I felt that these past years that I was always in the hall on October 16. I was always trying to get out while messages were being given to me (Christmas tree, Easter candle, and Transfigured Christ), but there was no human way out of this situation until the blond at the door with the face of St. Bridget opened the door for me. Then I would simply walk out and begin my work – whatever that might be. On the paper of October 15, I matched the blond at the door with "lucky." It was perfectly clear next week, the lucky numbers would come in, I would win the lottery, and this trial would be over.

I bought my ticket for the November 12 drawing. I couldn't turn on the television that night because I was too nervous. How many times had I convinced myself that all of the signs pointed to a particular day when I would be out of this mess, only to be disappointed later? I woke up the next morning and almost passed out. November 12 was my confirmation day when I took the name Paul after St. Paul. Now, this! Every number was selected except for my lucky number, 4. The number 4 had been my lucky number since I could remember. Instead, the number 35 was selected. The numbers were 7,11,14,19,23, 35. The disappointment completely overshadowed the fact that I did win some much-needed money. I looked at the ticket again, and there were three other numbers, 872. In exactly 872 hours, there would be another lottery drawing on Wednesday. Perhaps the 4 meant in four days. Wednesday, November 16 came, and my numbers did not come in.

CHAPTER 26

$$\text{———} \; \backsim \mathcal{UU} \backsim \; \text{———}$$

THE TRANSFIGURATION

OCTOBER 16, 1982, IN Vienna, I saw the Christmas tree, the Easter candle, and then the dazzling white Jesus. I knew it was Jesus since He was associated with the Christmas tree and Easter Candle. Each year on August 6, the church celebrates the feast of the Transfiguration:

> Jesus took with him Peter and the brothers James and John and led them up a high mountain where they were alone. As they looked on, a change came over Jesus; his face was shining like the sun, and his cloths were dazzling white. Then the three disciples saw Moses and Elijah talking to Jesus. So Peter spoke up and said to Jesus,

> 'Lord, how good it is that we are here! If you wish, I will make three tents here, one for you, one for Moses, and one for Elijah.' While he was talking, a cloud came over them, and a voice from the cloud said, 'This is my own dear son, with whom I'm pleased – listen to him!'

> When the disciples heard the voice, they were so terrified that they threw themselves facing downward to the ground. Jesus came to them and touched them. 'Get up; he said, 'Don't be afraid.' So they looked up, and no one was there but Jesus. As they came down the mountain, Jesus ordered them, 'Don't tell anyone about the vision you have seen until the Son of Man has been raised from death." (Matthew 17: 1-0).

At the baptism of Jesus, when He began His public life, the Father announced that Jesus was His son. At the transfiguration, there was the same announcement. He was to begin His final journey to death and glory in Jerusalem. The face shining like the sun and the dazzling white clothes pre-figure His future glory. Moses and Elijah were there as symbols of the law and the prophets. Jesus, in His glory, is the fulfillment of the law and the prophets.

I thought that the church picked a peculiar day to celebrate the transfigured Christ. August 6, 1945, was the day that the first nuclear bomb was dropped on Japan. This was the beginning of the nuclear age, and we have all been held hostage to the threat of nuclear destruction since that day.

CHAPTER 27

NOVEMBER 23, 1988

BY WEDNESDAY, NOVEMBER 23, 1988, I had recovered from the near miss in the lottery. I was again hopeful that today would be the day. I was wrong again. But, just like October 22, the numbers selected that night were interesting: 2,6,912,32,34. I didn't know why, but these numbers had a hidden meaning to me. 2 the body and blood or the second station of the cross, 34 Mary or Marcus the 34th pope. Today was the feast day of the fourth pope, Clement.

I had been going to this school since October, 1982. At this point, I would rather have a good hot meal than more signs.

CHAPTER 28

MAY AND JUNE, 1989

I NOTICED THAT THE other numbers on the lottery ticket that I bought for Saturday, May 13, 1989, were 2,6,9,12, and 32. The 34 already stood for May 13, the day Mary first appeared at Fatima. I was hopeful, and again, I was a loser. May 14 was mother's day, and it was also the feast day for Pentecost. I thought about last November 12 and the 35 substituting for 4, and I counted 39 more days to June 21, 1989. Perhaps that was the day? It wasn't the day, but at 4 PM, I was standing a foot from the door to my apartment. I was home, sick with a cold again, looking at something in the closet. The doorbell rang. I opened the door immediately. There was no one there. Shortly afterward, I was in the kitchen cleaning up when I turned to look at the hall for no apparent reason. Then the idea of "next week" came to me. I turned and looked at the clock and it was 4:14 PM. Next week on June 28, my numbers were going to come in at last.

On the seventh Friday after Easter, the church gospel reading is always John 21: 15-19. This is where Jesus asks Peter three times, "Do you love me?' and tells Peter to "feed my sheep." This is the same reading of the evening of June 28. June 29 is the feast day for Peter and Paul. The vigil reading on the evening of June 28 is John 21:15-19. It is the most unusual reading in the bible because there is an obvious mistake. The first question – "Do you love me?" is not that question but is "Do you love me more than the others?" Then the next two questions are: Do you love me? How could Peter possibly know if he loves Jesus more than, say, St. John? He can't. It might be argued that St. John loved Jesus more than any of the other apostles, as he was the only one standing at the cross with Mary. Then from the cross, Jesus announced that John was to be Mary's son and Mary was to be his mother. It might be that the phrase "more than these" was added later to emphasize the importance of the Pope. I'm going to use this gospel reading instead of John 14 and John 19 when I pray for people to be healed.

Because of the Palestinian uprising and because the Iran-Iraq war was over, Israel was in the Saudi Arabian news almost daily. A series of cables of congratulations or condolences between world leaders were reported. Two leaders would be shown together with music in the background while the newscaster would always announce the content of their discussion with the monotonous ever-present "bilateral relations were discussed." I had never heard an Arab leader speak. It was a combination of a silent movie with newscaster's voices. Communist Yemen had merged with its noncommunist counterpart, so Saudi Arabia no longer had a communist neighbor. Except for the Jews who had stolen Palestine, there was no one more despicable to the Saudi Arabians than the Godless communists. So all of these events, plus the Soviet withdrawal from Afghanistan and partial withdrawal from Europe, brought an increased sense of security to the area.

One day I was getting ready for work and noticed that my stethoscope was not in my white coat pocket. I had used it at the hospital yesterday afternoon. It didn't drop out of my pocket. None of the nurses or translators would have taken it. Saudi patients do not steal. So where was it? It would be difficult to replace because it was the same one I had used since graduating from medical school. I retraced my steps from the previous day and could not find it. Perhaps it was a sign similar to when my paycheck had disappeared. Later that day, I received my new one-year contract to sign. The Medical Director did not understand my sudden change of plans since, during the previous weeks, we had negotiated the contract, and I seemed to be pleased. He offered me a better deal, but I told him that it was just time for me to leave. I never did find the stethoscope. I prepared to leave as soon as I could get the exit visa. My "point of origin" was New York, so I would be given a first-class ticket to fly there. After that, I had no plans except to purchase a lottery ticket.

CHAPTER 29

───⟨⫸⟩───

BACK IN THE U.S.A

1990 WAS COMING TO an end, and I had decided to move to a suburb of Boston. I could use public transportation to the city, and I found a job pushing papers in a medical insurance company. My stethoscope was taken away, and I didn't miss seeing patients. The only absolute job requirement was that I had to live in a place that had a lottery. During my trip to interview for the job, I was assured that Massachusetts had two different lotteries each week. I asked if one of the lotteries had a drawing time of 9:58 PM and was told that each week on Wednesday and Saturday at that time six lottery numbers were selected. The other lottery was at 8 PM on Friday.

Growing up in the New York area gave me the feeling that Boston was to be pitied as a second-rate city. It was a big New England town that had to endure the Red Sox baseball team. Sure, it had the once mighty Celtics basketball team, but that was an aberration. Besides, Red Auerbach was more a New Yorker than a Bostonian. He had no Boston accent. He didn't park his car near the yard but smoked cigars and won championships like the New York Yankees. The same way that Rome did not recover from the destruction of the Roman Empire and will never reach those heights again, Boston will forever have to endure the "trade" of Babe Ruth to the New

York Yankees. The last time that the Red Sox won the World Series was when Babe Ruth pitched for them. He was the best left-handed pitcher in baseball and held several world series pitching records for a time, but it was the Yankees who realized that the Babe should be hitting baseballs every day, not pitching. Babe Ruth was and will forever be the greatest baseball player as a Hall of Fame pitcher and a Hall of Fame hitter. The Red Sox had him, and because their owner needed cash for a non-baseball-related investment (No No Nannette was a play he wanted to invest in), Babe Ruth was sold! Yes, he was traded to another team for cash. There was no reserve law in baseball at the time, and players had to keep playing for their team even if their contracts had expired. He would have been a Boston Red Sox player forever. Babe Ruth was sold for cash to the New York Yankees. A giant of a human being who became a bigger-than-life institution that could never be replaced was sold for a pile of dollars that had the same value and uniqueness as any other pile of dollars. Yankees stadium became the House that Ruth built. The Yankees were blessed, and the Red Sox were cursed (the curse of the Bambino). To those who have, even more, will be given. The Yankees were to get DiMaggio, Mantle, Ford, and a long list of great players and championships. The Red Sox also had some great players, but that was just to emphasize the curse. Their great players like Ted Williams would allow the Red Sox to get close enough to a championship so that they and their fans would experience even greater agony.

If your team is in last place, you lose interest in following them. However, if they are competing for the playoffs and a championship, they hold your attention. You begin to get involved with the race. Each game becomes important in the standings. In 1967 the Red Sox manager was asked who he would pitch in the seventh and deciding game, He was a good manager, and he had great players, including the best pitcher in the American League and the most valuable batter, so he replied, "Lonborg and champagne." Of course the Red Sox lost. Didn't he know that the Red Sox were supposed to lose to the St. Louis Cardinals? In 1975, the Red Sox won a dramatic sixth world series game in overtime (extra innings) only to lose to the Cincinnati Reds in the seventh game. In 1978, at the mid-season, the Red Sox were in the first place, fourteen games ahead of their nearest rival, the New York Yankees. In a dramatic drive, they managed to lose this overwhelming lead so that at the end of the season of 162 games, there would be a one-game playoff at Fenway Park in Boston to see who would go on to the World Series. Everyone on the entire planet "knew" that the Red Sox would lose to the New York Yankees. You could ask anyone in the jungles or deserts of the world, and if they ever heard the word baseball, they would tell you that the Red Sox were wasting their time. The Red Sox lost when Bucky Dent, a Yankee infielder who almost never hits a home run, hit a three-run homer to win the game.

The next time the Red Sox reached the World Series was in 1986 against the New York Mets. The Boston newspaper sports writers and fans were hopeful, but at least they "knew" that the Red Sox would lose. The question was how close the Red Sox would come to winning the World Series before the inevitable defeat occurred. Boston and New York sports programs were bombarded with suggestions of how the Red Sox would lose. What happened was beyond imagination. The Red Sox were ahead in games and won 3-2. They could actually afford to lose the sixth game before going on to lose the seventh game. Eventually, it came down to a key point at the end of the sixth game. The Mets were behind. Three more outs and the Red Sox would win the World Series. There was then tremendous pressure for the Red Sox to find a way to lose. The Mets got a couple of men on base but were down to their last out. In this last inning Bob Stanley came in to pitch for the Red Sox. He was a relief pitcher who had some good years for the Red Sox and now was his chance to pitch well and become a world series hero. He would not let down his teammates. He didn't; he pitched magnificently. He was practically perfect. So how could the Red Sox manage to lose? They had the lead and the pitcher brought in to protect the lead was great that day. Simple, that is, simple for the Red Sox. It was actually very easy for them. Stanley threw the ball toward the batter and the catcher dropped the ball. The runner on third came in to score and the game was now tied. The other runner advanced to scoring position. The New York fans, not as learned about the Red Sox tradition as the New England fans, went wild. This was fantastic to them. By now, most of the television sets in new England were turned off. Most people do not go to see an execution. It's sad enough when a human being dies, but you don't have to watch it. The official scorer ruled that Bob Stanley threw a wild pitch; that is, it was his fault that the catcher dropped the ball. He didn't. He just got the blame. The ball wasn't thrown in the dirt. It wasn't too high. The ball was not curving or knuckling through the air. The catcher did not have to lunge to get to the ball. No, the ball was not difficult to catch at all. For some reason, the catcher must have lost sight of the ball and dropped it. The ball bounced off his glove and went past him, allowing the Mets runner to score. The game was still tied, and the Red Sox had not lost yet. Moments later, the batter hit a slow ground ball to the first base fielder. He had to catch the ball and step on first base. He didn't have to catch the ball and hurry to throw it to a teammate. He just had to catch the ball. Unfortunately for the Red Sox, but fortunately for all of the scientists of the world because the Red sox not winning the world series was one of the natural laws of nature that they depended upon. The Red Sox first baseman was injured and was hobbling around in need of surgery. He had no business being on the field at that point in the game. He could barely take a few painful steps and bend over. So he tried, and the ball went through his legs. There was only one injured Red Sox fielder on the field that day and of course there were healthy Red Sox players in the dugout, but the ball found it's way to the outfield. The Mets won the game. Bob Stanley never pitched better but lost. The Red Sox came within one pitch to winning the World Series in the sixth game. You can't do better than that. That's the closest you can come to winning before losing.

The result of the seventh game was a mathematical certainty. If the Red Sox won the seventh game, how could you explain it? You could probably get odds of a million to one that the Red Sox would lose the seventh game. Why the Red Sox and Mets players had to show up for the seventh game reminded me of when Jesus was baptized.

"At that time, Jesus arrived from Galilee and came to John at the Jordan to be baptized by him. But John tried to make him change his mind. 'I ought to be baptized by you,' John said. 'and yet you have come to me.'

But Jesus answered him, 'Let it be done for now. For in this way, we shall do all that God requires.'

So John agreed. (Matthew 3:13-15).

I didn't think it was specifically written into the ball payer's contract, but it is expected that, barring injury, you are to show up to play out the seventh game. So the players had to play the seventh game. The Mets won. It wasn't close.

There is real psychological masochistic sickness among the Red Sox fans. A rational person would move the team to another city. The team could move to Rhode Island for instance. Their name could be changed to the New England Red Sox and win the championship. However, rational people are in short supply. Red Sox attendance is always high. People want to see the agony of defeat and how close the red Sox come before losing. The Red Sox can't do any better than when they lost to the Mets in 1986. They can't come any closer to winning before losing.

CHAPTER 30

ST. MATTHEWS CATHOLIC CHURCH

THE BEST PART OF being back in the United States was being able to attend Mass again. People travel all over the world to see the great monuments that man has made but few will take the time to visit Jesus each day. St. Matthews Church reminded me of St. Stephens in Vienna because they both had the same zig-zag pattern on the roof. This was the only physical similarity in structure. The Mass, of course, was the same, except the choir in Vienna was a lot better. Nothing disturbs my concentration more than the enthusiastic singer without a singing voice sitting behind me and spraying my neck with their saliva.

St. Matthew was a Jewish tax collector for the Romans. To the religious Jew at the time, one did not associate with the heathen (non-Jew), those who by choice were employed in activities that precluded celebrating the Sabbath (shepherds who usually had to work on the Sabbath) or obvious sinners whose life reflected their outright rejection of God (murderers, prostitutes). The tax collector for the Romans, who was known for extortion and vice, was a unique combination of everything that was repulsive to the religious Jew. Hence the call of Matthew:

> "Jesus left that place and as he walked along, he saw a tax collector, named Matthew sitting in his office. He said to him, 'Follow me.' Matthew got up and followed him. While Jesus was having a meal in Matthew's house, many tax collectors and other outcasts came and joined Jesus and his disciples at the table. Some Pharisees saw this and asked his disciples, 'Why does your teacher eat with those people?' Jesus heard them and answered, 'People who are well don't need a doctor, but only those who are sick. Go and find out what is meant when the scripture says that it is kindness that I want, not animal sacrifices." (Matthew 9: 9-13).

People are chosen by God to do His will. He chooses us. St. Matthew was called and responded immediately. There are four gospels about the life and teachings of Jesus. Mark, Matthew, and Luke are similar in orientation and are called the Synoptic gospels. John, the other gospel is more theological. Luke wrote in Greek. He was a physician, a traveling companion of St. Paul, and the only gentile writer of the New Testament. Mark wrote to the Roman world and was a frequent companion of St. Peter. John's concepts of Jesus as the word of God, Jesus as the light of the world, God as love, Jesus as the food of life, and the gift of the Holy Spirit make him the theological writer to all Christians. But it was Matthew, the repulsive Jewish outcast, who wrote to God's chosen people. It is in the Gospel of Matthew that the teachings of Jesus are emphasized:

> "Happy are those who know they are spiritually poor; the kingdom of heaven belongs to them.

> Happy are those who mourn; God will comfort them.

> Happy are those who are humble; they will receive what God has promised.

> Happy are those whose greatest desire is to do what God requires; God will satisfy them fully.

Happy are those who are merciful to others; God will be merciful to them.

Happy are the pure in heart; they will see God

Happy are those who work for peace; God will call them his children.

Happy are those who are persecuted because they do what God requires;

The kingdom of heaven belongs to them.

Happy are you when people insult you and persecute you and tell all kinds of lies against you because

You are my followers. Be happy and glad. For a great reward is kept for you in heaven. This is how the

Prophets who lived before you were persecuted." (Matthew 5:3-12).

God is the great re-creator. Matthew was chosen to be an instrument of His will. Peter denied God, and Paul persecuted His followers. God likes to take the instruments of the Devil (the cross) and turn them into symbols of His love (the cross). Each day God waits for the sinner to turn to Him. Each day brings a new opportunity to repent. One's past mistakes are not insurmountable in the quest for heaven. We should not be too discouraged about our imperfect past transgressions, but through the grace of Jesus, God will forgive, provided you forgive others.

CHAPTER 31

———◦⟊◦———

EASTER, 1991

I HAD MY USUAL routine again. I got up, went to church, went to work, bought my lottery tickets, threw out the losing lottery tickets, and started again. I did not understand why there were two new visionaries in Medjugorje. The analogy between Fatima and Medjugorje was now disrupted. Then I again read the story of May 13, 1917, when Mary first met the three children at Fatima. After the request for the children to return on the thirteenth of each month until October, Mary told them that she would return a seventh time. Perhaps she was promising to come one more time to Fatima. Perhaps this seventh visit had already occurred. She appeared to them many times after October 13, 1917. If I was correct with my analogy to Medjugorje, the appearance of Mary to the two new visionaries there meant that the message of Fatima would come to another person who was not one of the original visionaries. There were three children at Fatima, and there were six children at Medjugorje. Then there were two new ones at Medjugorje, so there had to be one new one for Fatima. Everything else matched perfectly.

Father Meehan, the pastor of St. Matthews church, was always busy. He had been ordained thirty-three years ago and was an enthusiastic, intelligent, and thoroughly likable priest. He always had a tasteful joke or witty comment for the parishioners. People would smile as he approached to get ready to laugh. He must have had his faults like us. I couldn't find any except for the curse of New England; he was a Red Sox fan. I kept telling him that he was wasting his time praying for them to win the world series. He kept telling me that he was a man of faith and that although it appeared hopeless, all things were possible with God. Just for Father Meehan's sake, I, too, hoped that the Red Sox would win the world series. They had broken his heart so many times. Was I beginning to get infected with this Red Sox illness?

Easter was approaching. 1991 was a great year for me so far. I was back in the US, going to church without starving. On Easter Sunday, St. Matthew's Church was beautiful. The Easter Lilies were all over the church. The church was packed full of us sinners. Father Meehan introduced his friend, Father Merril, who was visiting from Karlsruhe, Germany. Father Merril lit the Easter candle. Karlsruhe, I knew there was something about it. I kept thinking about it all through the mass. After Mass, I kept thinking about it and sat in the church for a while as it emptied. I felt guilty about not concentrating at Mass. The church was empty. A little old man was tidying up the pews. He left, and I was alone with the Easter candle providing some light. The little old man returned dragging a Christmas tree, one of those artificial metal ones. He stopped as he walked by, saying to himself, more than to me, that this decoration was for the wrong season and belonged in the basement.

Suddenly I jumped out of my seat and ran home. I found the newspaper and looked up the lottery numbers. THERE IT WAS! 4,7,11,14,19,23! It may have been Holy Week, but I had purchased my ticket on Saturday, and I was out of the hall! Karlsruhe was where the retired American soldier in the carriage to Neuschwanstein was stationed. I met him on October 15, 1982. The Christmas tree and Easter candle were shown to me on October 16, 1982, in the hall before seeing Jesus. I knelt down and prayed that God would continue to lead me with His Holy Spirit.

The next day I went to Braintree, a small town south of Boston, to collect my lottery winnings as the only jackpot winner. After the money was withheld for taxes, I received the first of my annual checks for $91,414.34 after taxes. After depositing my check, I called in at work and told them that I was resigning immediately. I was smiling, laughing and was so happy. I wasn't hallucinating the bells, numbers, or lights. I was definitely not insane. I was now eccentric. A few days later, I purchased a suit, shoes, traveler's checks, and a plane ticket to Portugal.

CHAPTER 32

FATIMA, PORTUGAL

I WAS NOW ON a thirty-year pension. Financially independent, I was now free to do whatever I was called to do. As I was flying to Portugal, I tried to figure out what the remaining two signs symbolized. There was still the Frauenkirche, Our Lady's cathedral church in Munich, and the Residence, the home of the Wittlesbach royal family of Bavaria, to explain. They were both marked on the map of Munich on October 15, 1982.

The plane landed in Lisbon, and then I traveled to Fatima. I started to visit the cathedral at Fatima. The original church had been destroyed by dynamite in 1922 and was rebuilt. The devotion of the pilgrims was evident. I visited the place Mary visited the children on May 13, 1917. I visited the place she met the children on August 19, 1917. There was also the spot where the angel gave the children communion before Mary appeared. There were some sick pilgrims who requested help. We are told to persevere in prayer even when our requests are not granted:

> "Jesus left that place and went off to the territory near the cities of Tyre and Sidon. A Canaanite woman who lived in that region came to him, 'Son of David,' she cried out, 'Have mercy on me, sir. My daughter has a demon and is in a terrible condition.' But Jesus

did not say a word to her. His disciples came to him and begged him. 'Send her away. She is following us and making all this noise.'

Jesus replied, 'I have been sent only to the lost sheep of the people of Israel.'

At this, the woman came and fell at his feet. 'Help me, sir,' she said.

Jesus answered, 'It is not right to take the children's food and throw it to the dogs.'

'That's true, sir,' she answered, 'but even the dogs eat the leftovers that fall from their master's table.

So Jesus answered her, 'You are a woman of great faith! What you want will be done for you.'

At that moment, her daughter was healed." (Matthew 15: 21-28).

I kept praying for direction. I was free, out of the enclosed hall, but I wasn't sure how to proceed. I stayed a couple of days and started thinking about leaving. I didn't have any plans and didn't know where to go.

CHAPTER 33

DEMONS

IN BIBLICAL TIMES PEOPLE explained sickness as the result of the Devil and demons. If you were sick, you had a demon. As man became more knowledgeable and sophisticated, he realized that the cause of illness could be infections, a poor diet, or exposure to toxins. There were no demons, just cardiovascular disease from too much cholesterol and fats. There were no demons, just emphysema, lung cancer, and vascular disease from smoking cigarettes. These were the real demons: germs, toxins, and cigarette smoke.

When a twentieth-century man reads a part of the bible in which Jesus is healing someone and exorcising demons, he may interpret this to mean that Jesus is healing someone (performing a miracle) and explaining it to the people in terms that they can understand. See, Jesus didn't believe in demons either? He was just using demons to explain to the sick person in terms that they could understand. While this may make sense to modern man, it is not correct. Jesus did believe in the Evil One and demons. He saw the devil thrown out of heaven. He conversed with the Evil One and was tempted by him. He was taken to the top of the temple and told to jump by the Evil One. The Evil One quoted psalm 91 to Him.

When Jesus healed someone, He was not putting on an act by implying that the demon was exorcised because people in biblical times were ignorant of modern science. They may not have been knowledgeable as your average biochemistry Nobel Laureate, but they understood that lepers could spread their disease and had to be isolated from the community.

CHAPTER 34

THE VISION

After five days in Fatima, it was time to leave. I prayed the rosary at each of the places of importance. I went to Mass, I went to confession and I prayed the Stations of the Cross. As a sick pilgrim expecting a miracle and not receiving one, I was confused. I was certain that I would receive some message at Fatima. I packed my suitcase, found my passport and was about to leave my room and go to Lisbon when the face of a beautiful lady appeared. Her hair was covered. Her blue eyes poured out of the perfect features of her face.

"Where are you going?" she asked.

"I don't know," I answered as I kneeled down.

"The Holy Father is to consecrate Russia to my Immaculate Heart together with the bishops of the church in the Cathedral Church of the Immaculate Conception in Moscow. They are to bring in the Icon of Our Lady of Vladimir for the consecration. Also, the Church of the Holy Family in Barcelona is to be completed. This must be done to prevent the nuclear holocaust.

"How am I to do this?" I asked.

"Pray the rosary; my immaculate heart will help you," she replied and was gone.

I took the rosary out of my pocket and prayed. So that is what I had been prepared for all of these years. If I had only seen her face and heard her message, I would have dismissed this as a hallucination. Now everything made perfect sense. The Residence was where the Wittlesbach Bavarian royalty lived. The Frauenkirche was near the residence. It was the main cathedral church of Munich named for Our Lady. The last piece of the puzzle was the set of numbers: 2,6,9,12,32,34. The 2 is the second Station of the Cross, and the 9 is the ninth mystery of the rosary. In both, Jesus takes up the cross. The 12 represents noon when the three children of Fatima met Mary, 34. The visionaries of Fatima were told of the start of World War II. Perhaps the secret that the visionaries of Medjugorje were living with all these years was an impending worldwide nuclear holocaust, World War III.

I unpacked my suitcase and went back to the cathedral to pray. I knew what had to be done but had no idea where to begin. I also did not know how much time was left to prevent the unthinkable.

CHAPTER 35

WHERE TO GO?
WHAT TO DO?

WHY DIDN'T I ASK her if I was going to heaven? Heaven is everything to me. Why didn't I ask her when I had a chance? Of Course, I'm going to heaven. All of the people who are given assignments like this go to heaven. All of the ones in the bible went to heaven. Actually, we only know about the ones who were successful. What about the ones who were given a message and were not successful in their work? We never hear of them. For most of the twentieth century, people have been raising money to complete the Church of the Holy Family in Barcelona, and it still didn't have a roof or completed walls. I don't have the luxury of waiting for another century.

I sat there and tried to think of the various courses of action. First, why would anyone listen to me? I'm not an important person. A routine check of my background would reveal that I haven't been able to hold a job for longer than a year or two. Have you ever seen the average physician at a social gathering? They are the least socially adept group of professionals on the planet. If you stop them from speaking about anything related to medicine, most of them can't carry on a conversation. Invariably they would bring the conversation back to a medically related field. It's a little like the old Mutual of Omaha commercials on Wild Kingdom. The narrator would start talking about some African animal and then, through some deft analogy that I could never understand, bring the audience to the topic of insurance for the commercial.

I could go to Medjugorje and speak to one of the visionaries. They might listen to me and help me. However, they already have their work with millions of pilgrims who hound them to death. They don't need me to complicate their already harried life.

I could go to the Central Intelligence Agency (CIA). I'm an American citizen. They're concerned with the security of the United States and the world. They might be interested in preventing a nuclear war. The CIA would certainly have the influence and means to finish the walls and roof of the Holy Family church in Barcelona. So I should go to Washington, walk into their main building, and ask for whom? Say what? If I started telling my story, how long would I last before they thought I was a lunatic? If I want people to laugh at me, why don't I try comedy?

I could go to the Department of State and perhaps last a few minutes longer than at the CIA before they threw me out. They're not as smart as the people at the CIA. They take the reports from the CIA, consult their specialists and talk to influential people around the world and then come up with deft policies like, "Let's send in the United States Marines to Lebanon to maintain peace." Never mind that Lebanon does not exist and that the area has factions that are actively killing each other. Forget that there are fully equipped armies at war in the area and that most of these armies have no relations with the United States. Peace is a noble goal, but sending in the marines is suicide. Maybe I might last a whole hour at the State Department.

I could go to Rome and try to meet the Pope. Can you imagine the Holy Father listening to me tell him stories about bells, lights, and lottery numbers? I could tell him about the message that I received and what he must do in union with the bishops in Moscow. He probably gets advice from thousands of the faithful. He doesn't know me, and if he did, he certainly wouldn't believe me. If not immediately thrown out and labeled a lunatic, I might be referred to a commission, and in a few years, a report would be filed and placed in a vault. Probably the only way anyone would see the report would be after the nuclear catastrophe blasted the vault apart and into the atmosphere. I need the help of the Vatican and the United States government. It is time to go home and start seeing Cardinal O'Connor of New York and Cardinal Law of Boston to get to the Vatican.

CHAPTER 36

THE CARDINALS WHO FLY

IN MY TRAVELS OF employment, I've had the privilege of listening to both Cardinal O'Connor and Cardinal Law give sermons. The strength of their character, the sincerity of their faith, their intelligence, and their public speaking ability are immediately evident. They must administer to large dioceses, be active in international church affairs, be involved in local and national political affairs, and continue to nourish their own spiritual lives.

So why would they have any more time for me than the Pope, CIA, or State Department? It would be difficult to talk to them. How I'll convince them will have to wait for later. Once I get to the talking stage, I'll be alright. After all, we each work for the same boss and are accountable to Him. I'm being led by the Holy Spirit, and they're open to the Holy Spirit, so something should work out.

How will I know if they are even in the country? Both of them travel. John Cardinal O'Connor made a well-meaning trip to Israel. It made sense for him to go there. The Holy Land shouldn't be off-limits for a Cardinal. He is the Cardinal of a city with the world's largest Jewish population. Jews and the Catholic church have had terrible relations for hundreds of years, so why not do something to improve these relations? The Jews feel that the Christians and

Catholic church have persecuted them. In the annals of history, who was more of an antisemite than the Catholic church or Martin Luther? Pope John Paul II was the first Pope to attend a service in a Roman synagogue, so perhaps relations were improving. However, the Catholic church did not recognize the state of Israel at the time. If ever there was a country that the sons of Mary should have cordial relations with, it is with the country of the Star of David. Those defending the Catholic church will say that they do not recognize the state of Israel because of some convoluted policy on Jerusalem, that Jerusalem should be an international city. Or perhaps they will refer to the fact that the boundaries of the State of Israel are not set in the eyes of a large part of the world. That policy and that kind of thinking are preposterous. There are boundary disputes between countries and movements of independence within countries all around the world, and the Catholic church sends its ambassadors to many of these countries. While Jerusalem is a holy spiritual city to the Christians, Jews, and moslems, it is also a physical city like any other. The garbage must be collected. Security must be maintained. The government of Israel has provided access to Jerusalem for pilgrims of any religion. What more should the Catholic church demand? Jews are God's chosen people. They are His children too. The Moslems are the older brothers of the Jews because they are the sons of Ishmael. The Christians are His adopted sons. There should be no reason for hatred in this heavenly family except for those who intent on doing the will of the Evil One.

John Cardinal O'Connor made his pilgrimage to Israel in good faith as a man who was trying to improve the cause of peace. For his trouble, he had to endure the official public reprimand of the Vatican diplomatic corp and the criticism of various American Jewish groups. He did his best, but round one went to the Evil One. Hopefully, there will be a round two and another trip. If you had to pick two American cardinals who were closest to the Pope and they seemed to have a unique relationship with President Bush, it made sense to get these two cardinals to bring me to the Pope and the President.

CHAPTER 37

ROUND ONE, BOSTON

I WAS BACK IN my apartment trying to devise a plan to get Cardinal Law to help me. As busy as Cardinal Law was, I noticed that he always found time to preside at the funeral mass of a priest. He was concerned about his priests and was a good shepherd. I decided that I was not going to tell anyone about the lights, the bells, or the lottery numbers. What had to be done was important, not how I knew what had to be done. My message and authority were from God and from Mary, but no one would listen to me unless they were given a reason to listen. The only thing I knew how to do was how to pray. I had been taught how to pray and had been given oil consecrated for the sick. I was looking for someone who was sick with an incurable disease, who was not actively being treated so that the miraculous nature of the healing was evident, and who was well known to the cardinal. What I needed was a sick priest who the cardinal knew very well. After a few days of trying to learn more about Cardinal Law I noticed in the obituary page of the Boston Globe that funeral services were going to be held tomorrow for Father Hardiman of Lowell and that the cardinal would preside.

I was early. I had my rosary, my bible, and the oil. Many priests started to arrive. Each was sullen, but they appeared in good health.

Relatives of Father Hardiman and more friends came into the church. The Mass started, and I looked around the church until I spotted a priest sitting in a wheelchair. He looked about sixty-five years old and appeared to have some difficulty speaking. I thought he had a stroke since he couldn't move his left arm or left leg. I moved closer to him. I was right; he couldn't move his left side. Now the important question was how long he had been in this condition. If he had the stroke last week, it could be argued that part of the natural course of his illness was an improvement. However, if his condition was chronic and stable, then the miraculous nature of the healing would be obvious. I asked one of the other priests, who told me that the man in the wheelchair was Father Dayton, who had suffered a stroke three years ago. Father Dayton used to teach at the seminary and was well known to the Cardinal and most of the priests of Boston. He lived in a retirement home. I had all of the information I needed.

The next day I called the retirement home and spoke to Father Dayton. He had difficulty speaking and understanding me. I introduced myself and asked if he would mind if I visited him tomorrow. He told me that except for his physical therapy at one o'clock, he would be free until three, when he always prayed the rosary. He stated that all of his meetings had been cancelled. He still had a good sense of humor. I told him that I would meet him at 9:58 AM and that he'd better not be late. He chuckled and hung up the phone.

I walked into his room the next morning and started to pray for him as I had been taught. I said the readings, and then when I anointed his forehead with the holy oil, he was miraculously cured. He could move perfectly. He had no difficulty speaking. Both of us were so happy. As I left, I asked him to tell Cardinal Law and have the cardinal call me with the phone number I gave him.

CHAPTER 38

LUNCH WITH THE CARDINAL

THAT EVENING I RECEIVED a call from the Cardinal's residence. I was invited to the residence to have lunch with Cardinal Law the next day. I told the priest on the phone that I would be happy to attend. It seemed too easy.

I arrived at the residence about twenty minutes early. I was wearing my only good suit with my best tie and new shoes. As I was led into his office, I said the Hail Mary to myself. We shook hands, and he told me that lunch would be ready in about ten minutes. We would be joined by four priests. I told him that lunch wouldn't be necessary, that I didn't want a lot of people to see me here, and that I had an urgent message for the Pope and for President Bush. I asked for his help. But first, I needed him to find a chronically sick priest who Cardinal O'Connor knew very well. I asked Cardinal Law to get a good history of the patient and to go with me to meet the patient and Cardinal O'Connor. I told him that if the priest was recently discharged from the hospital, there would be a discharge summary that would be useful. Then I left.

I was worried about being rude to the cardinal. I didn't want a lot of people knowing about me. I didn't trust myself, let alone other people. Look, I've lived forty years without eating lunch with the cardinal, so what If I Never Get Invited Back?

CHAPTER 39

——✦——

ROUND TWO, NEW YORK

I DID NOT BELIEVE that whoever I prayed for would be healed by God. I was certain that in the circumstance of praying for someone to help me accomplish the mission, God would hear my prayers and grant my request. I could not wake up tomorrow and heal everyone and clear out of the hospital. Furthermore, where there is grace and a mission to do God's will, there is also the Evil One attempting to interfere with those plans. The Evil One already caused me to wait from June 28, 1989, to Easter 1991.

I was thinking about this a week after meeting with Cardinal Law when the phone rang. It was Cardinal Law. He told me that a suitable patient had been identified and that he had a recent hospital discharge summary of the patient. He asked if I wanted to see the summary before he arranged for the meeting with the patient and Cardinal O'Connor. I told him that I would pick it up later in the day.

I picked up the envelope, brought it back to my apartment, and began to read it. Father Benjamin was forty-seven years old. Five years ago, he was in the wrong place at the wrong time. He was driving home on the highway at night when a twenty-two-year-old intoxicated driver got onto the same highway the wrong way against the traffic. There was a head-on collision that left Father Benjamin comatose since that time. He was maintained on a ventilator, was unresponsive to painful stimuli, and was recently discharged from a hospital where he had been treated for pneumonia. He was perfect! Poor Father Benjamin was barely alive. I told Cardinal Law to set up the meeting.

Next week Cardinal Law and I flew to New York. I told him that I was still nervous about flying. The planes were getting older; there was greater traffic congestion in the air, and every few months, you read about another tragedy or near miss. Here we were, traveling to a comatose patient expecting a miracle, and the "man of God" was fidgeting about going up in an airplane. I have faith in god, but unfortunately, he was not flying that day. Instead, there was an old pilot with grey hair and a large red nose who walked down the aisle. The ride went smoothly, and a car was waiting for us at the airport.

Cardinal Law and I arrived to find Cardinal O'Connor praying near the patient. All of us were heartbroken at the sight of Father Benjamin. The patient was connected to a respirator with a tube from his neck, a tracheostomy tube. There was a feeding bag that fed him via a tube connected to his stomach, a gastric tube, or a G tube. There was a tube in his bladder to collect the urine. There was little muscle mass left after five years of atrophy. A few bed sores, and pressure sores, were evident enough.

I took out my rosary, bible, and oil. I asked the Cardinals for their blessing. Then I started to pray the way I had been taught to pray since October 15, 1982. As soon as I finished anointing Father Benjamin with the oil, he was cured! He could move all of his muscles, but he couldn't speak. Both of the cardinals were astounded. They had never seen anything like this, and neither had I. All of us were crying. We all praised God. Poor Father Benjamin was so grateful, but he wanted to say something and couldn't speak. I tried to explain that the respirator was connected to the patient via the tracheostomy tube in his neck. The tube was below his vocal cords. The air went back and forth from the ventilator to his lungs, bypassing the vocal cords, and that was why he could not speak.

I asked a nurse to find a respiratory therapist who might be able to help us. He came into the room and was shocked to see the patient moving. Then I watched as the therapist disconnected the ventilator and easily extubated the patient. The patient could now speak. I explained to the nurse and to the respiratory therapist that both Cardinals had prayed for the patient, which was true, and now the patient was cured.

Within two days, the G tube and all of the other tubes were removed. His stomach was surgically repaired. He would still look emaciated for a couple of months, but he was in perfect health. God cures directly and indirectly.

CHAPTER 40

THE CARDINALS WERE ON MY SIDE

AFTER LEAVING FATHER BENJAMIN, we went to Cardinal O'Connor's residence in New York City.

Cardinal Law and I had tickets to fly back to Boston that evening, but there was much to discuss before our return trip. They kept asking me questions about myself. They wanted to know who I was and what I wanted from them. I refused to answer any questions about myself after the first few questions. I was a man who was given a job to do. The job was very important; I wasn't. They didn't have to know anything else about me except to contact me should the need arise. I didn't tell them about bells, lottery numbers, or lights. I did tell them the message I received from the Blessed Virgin Mary. I told them what had to be done and the consequences of failure. I also told them that besides arranging for a visit with the Pope, it would be important to get the United States government involved. They could provide more intensive security for the Pope and provide help completing the Sacred Family Church in Barcelona. They could help with the complicated political maneuvering that would be necessary to get the Pope and bishops to Moscow. I finally realized that I had to attend the consecration, and as a US citizen, the government could help me. Previously I thought I did not have to be present at the consecration. There were four bells on July 10, 1987. First at the seventh station (by the grace of God), then in St. Stephens Episcopal Church, then in my car (I would be traveling there), and finally in my office (this was my job). Again, I did not tell the Cardinals how I knew this; I just explained what had to be done. After seeing what happened to Father Benjamin and being open to the spirit of God, they did not need any other evidence. There was no better combination of faith and intelligence than present in both Cardinal Law and Cardinal O'Connor. I was astounded by what these two great men could accomplish in a matter of days.

CHAPTER 41

—⌒◇⫘◇⌒—

WASHINGTON D.C.

DESPITE THE PRESIDENT'S BUSY schedule, two weeks later, I found myself at a meeting with President Bush, Vice President Quayle, Director of the CIA Webster, and the National Security Director Scowcroft. Each had been made familiar with the literature about Fatima and Medjugorje prior to the meeting. The Cardinals brought in Father Benjamin to give a testimonial. He still had a small button hole in his neck from the tracheostomy tube and the recent surgical scars to repair his stomach and remove the G tube. He also presented slides of his medical record, and a couple of pictures were taken during his illness. The Cardinals had prepared everything. I just sat there and listened.

After his presentation, Father Benjamin left the meeting, and Cardinal Law explained what had happened in Fatima, the prophecies of Fatima, and what was presently occurring at Medjugorje. Then Cardinal O'Connor reviewed what had to be done.

President Bush was then the first to speak. He wanted a complete list of all the people who had to be present at the consecration in Russia to be given to CIA Director Webster. President Bush said that the number one priority of the US government was to see that the Cardinals had what they needed. He also said that immediate steps should be taken to provide security for the individuals who had to attend the consecration. He also promised funding to complete the cathedral in Barcelona. Secretary of State Baker was to contact his Russian counterpart and set up a meeting with President Gorbachev.

For the next hour, there was a general discussion about Fatima and Medjugorje. I was amazed at the intelligent questions that were being asked. Apparently, the CIA had a special unit assigned to investigations of prophecy, supernatural events, and religion. Religion was their business. Everything that might affect the security of the United States was their business. The Secretary of State said that I would b provided a diplomatic passport. I was to learn that the CIA already knew everything about me. They looked through my apartment, tapped my phone, and investigated my pathetic work history. The only question that I was asked during the meeting was whether Cardinal O'Connor was accurate in his report of what had to be done. He was. At the end of the meeting, James Baker asked if I might visit a sick relative who was visiting Washington and who was dying of cancer. I always had my rosary in my pocket, and whenever I traveled, I brought my bible and the holy oil. I was ready. I knew there would be some test set up to convince the skeptical ones. Mr. Baker had delivered his lines on cue and with sincerity. The Cardinals were flying back after the meeting. Hotel arrangements were already made for me. I would be taken to see the patient that evening and fly back to Boston the next day.

A few hours later, two men arrived at my hotel room to escort me to the patient. I walked into a suburban home to find Mr. Frank Tandler and his wife eating a snack. I asked about his diagnosis and treatment. Mr. Tandler did not look like he had responded favorably to the chemotherapy. He was jaundiced (yellow), emaciated, and weak. His abdomen was swollen with fluid and cancer. He was sixty-nine years old going on a hundred and nine. A typed medical report was handed to me. It summarized his history, lab results, and surgical procedures. He had not received any recent chemotherapy because of bone marrow suppression and infections. All he said was, "Thank you for coming. Please help me."

So I began to pray. I didn't care that the government was using this dying man as a sign, to believe me. He was probably an enthusiastic volunteer. He had nothing to lose. All I saw before me was a suffering, dying man who was enslaved by the Evil One. After I prayed and anointed him, the look on his face changed. There was a glow, an energy about him. He was no longer jaundiced! He was no longer in pain. He excused himself to urinate and announced that his abdomen was no longer distended.

He asked if this meant that the cancer was gone. I said that I believed that it was but that we should do some more tests to verify this. I knew that the government would provide further medical care. I told him that the only way to check was to repeat some of the tests. He replied that he would rather die first! That caught me by surprise. He was thinking of surgical exploration, bone marrow biopsies, and similar invasive procedures that had been done previously. I was thinking of taking some simple blood tests. I waited for the results of the blood tests, and an hour later, all of the results were normal. He felt fine and was cured. He thanked me, and I left.

CHAPTER 42

BACK HOME IN BOSTON

I HAD PERFORMED FOR them. When I returned to my hotel room, there was a packet on my bed. It contained my US diplomatic passport, information about a trade conference in Munich, and a plane ticket to Boston. I didn't like them making plans for me. The only person I had to see was the Pope, and he was in Italy, not Munich. I wanted to revisit Munich, Vienna, and Jerusalem one day, but right now, I wasn't interested in going on a tour. My only responsibility was to attend the consecration. I wanted to pray, go to church, and start a family when this was all over. Since I won the lottery, I have had dates with several attractive women. I could now interact normally. I didn't have a job, but most people could understand that winning the lottery was a good substitute. I was ready to settle down because I was happy and convinced of my sanity.

I boarded the plane to Boston the next day and was surprised to be directed to first class. I didn't realize I had a first-class ticket. I had never been in first class. The seats were wide, and more importantly, there was plenty of legroom. I had a seat next to the window and was looking out of it when I heard someone sit down next to me. It was the answer to any man's most fantastic dream. She was about five feet eight inches tall, had large beautiful blue eyes, long straight golden blond hair, perfect teeth, a thin athletic figure, and a fantastic smile that lit up the entire plane. I would learn during the flight that she was Marybeth Kennedy, who had a Ph.D. in biochemistry, worked at MIT and was twenty-five years old, and was never married. She had a great sense of humor and was very easy to converse with. Before I asked, she told me that she was not related to the Kennedys of Massachusetts. I told her I knew that because every picture I had ever seen of Ted Kennedy and Joe Kennedy showed that they were in dire need of a haircut and that her hair appeared neat and well-trimmed. She smiled and asked if I wanted to visit her lab. I declined the invitation saying that, as a physician, I would be out of place there. She countered that physicians were scientists. I told her that we were more like technicians. Then she criticized my false modesty.

I may not be the smartest person in the world, but I have learned in all of my years of waiting that I should never trust myself. I should only trust the Holy Spirit. Since I should never trust myself, it follows that I should never trust anyone else – Pope, president, cardinal, government official, or beautiful woman who happens to be sitting next to me. A man could not be trusted. The person sitting next to me was placed there. I was sure that I would see her again. She was placed there by someone who knew I was traveling on that flight and sitting in that seat. That left only three possibilities: the government, God, or the Evil One. She asked me if I liked to travel. Then before I could answer, she told me that her favorite place in the world was Munich, Germany. She started raving about the Deutsches Museum there. It was on an island in the Isar River that ran through Munich. It was the world's greatest science and technology museum. I'm sure Marybeth Kennedy was right. She went on and on about Munich, but I wasn't listening. I was too busy praying for my soul.

CHAPTER 43

THE APARTMENT IN BOSTON

Now that I was a known quantity to the CIA, little things began to change around me. Although I could never detect anyone following me, I was certain that I was being followed. They had to be following me because they had no choice. That was their job for the moment. I was important to them. If I didn't show up at the consecration, there would be a nuclear war. All of the nuclear weapons in the world would be launched by themselves or explode in place for some of them. There would be no human to initiate the launching process. Just like the bells and the lights without people turning them on or off and like the computer on November 13, 1987, following its own program, the missiles would be launched by the supernatural via a computer virus. The Evil One would use the end product of man's attempt to destroy himself to cause ultimate pain, suffering, and death.

The couple in the apartment across the hall moved out, and an enormous man moved in. He must have been about six feet six inches tall and weighed over two hundred and fifty pounds. The day after I returned home, I was visited by two men in expensive suits. They told me that they worked for the government, but I didn't believe them and told them to get lost. They then identified themselves as friends of the two men who had escorted me to Mr. Tandler, so I should believe them. I was just not in the mood to be escorted for the rest of my life and was giving them a difficult time.

I received a phone call from Cardinal Law about fifteen minutes later, saying that next week, we would be going to Rome. He also informed me that I might want to talk to the two men who had just left my apartment. I thanked him for his advice, hung up the phone, and tried to control my temper. I was angry.

The two men returned. We reviewed my life story; that is, they told me about myself. They had all the facts, including my elementary school report cards. There were psychological evaluations of my dead parents and a psychological report of how I might adjust to my new position in life. I was being volunteered to enter the group of marginally sane in need of constant observation. Perhaps I was already being treated? They could always tamper with my food. They asked me why I suddenly started to get all A's in third grade when I appeared to be struggling in the first and second grades. I told them that during the third grade, my parents finally bought me the Winky-dink piece of plastic that was placed over the television set so that I could color with the television characters. Prior to that, I would draw directly onto the television screen. This led to increased family tensions and screaming when my mother attempted to watch "I Love Lucy." The psychological stress was not inducive to my excelling in school. They were not amused. I told them that my elementary school grades were none of their business. They asked me why I was lying to them because I did have a Winky-dink plastic in second grade. They had interviewed some of my former playmates. Right there, I knew I was in for a long afternoon.

They offered me a very well-paying job. I told them that although I was out of work, I wasn't looking for any employment. They countered that they liked the way I handled myself during my flight home from Washington. I told them that I was certain that Miss Kennedy would have given me a highly technical tour of her lab at MIT but that I wasn't interested in a babysitter. One of them asked if I was asexual. I assured him that as soon as my life became normal, I would like to start a family but that my main concern always was to get to heaven. There was nothing on this earth; Miss Kennedy included, worth the risk of losing heaven. I asked them if they were getting a pay incentive because being concerned with my life must be very boring. They assured me that there was a great deal of extra compensation they were receiving to put up with me. It was a little bit like when they were assigned to eat at an expensive French restaurant; they would be reimbursed for the expense of the extra food that they had to order after they left the restaurant still hungry. They left, saying that they would be back with two other people tomorrow. I said that my apartment was too small to fit five people. They replied that they knew the size of my apartment and would take care of the details.

The next day they returned, and we drove to a private restaurant in Boston. We went into a private room. Seated alone was a slim, well-built man in his forties who was their boss. He started some small talk about how well Mr. Tandler was doing. I interrupted by telling him that I wasn't interested in discussing Mr. Tandler, eating at this restaurant, or wasting my time. He didn't change the smile on his face; it was permanently plastered on. He continued to flatter me, saying that the company (CIA) needed more people like me.

He offered me a job doing nothing for a million dollars a year. All I had to do was cooperate with security. They were just doing what the President had ordered. They were making certain that I was healthy, happy, and available. I would attend the consecration, and then they would leave me alone. I replied that the million dollars should be given to feed the hungry people of New York and Boston and that I was already cooperating with them. He asked me what I would do in his place. I told him that I had enough problems of my own, let's exchange places and try to solve his problems. He was far superior to me in intelligence. He was a big boy and could solve his own problems. He smiled and never lost a beat. I could have been the most despicable combination of Hitler and Stalin, and he probably would have smiled, continued undaunted, and complimented me on my advanced killing techniques. There was no doubt about it; he was a gem to behold. We were getting nowhere.

Miss Kennedy was brought in to join us. He started to introduce us when I interrupted to mention that we all knew that we had already met. I was becoming more rude as the conversation progressed. He told me that I was the most important person in the world and that they were not going to take any unnecessary chances with my security. I argued that he was wrong. The most important person was the Pope. He said that their evaluation suggested that the Pope and I were equally important. The two of us were the only people who had to attend the consecration; everyone else could be replaced. The Russians would take care of the security of the icon and the church. The icon was to be removed and replaced by a copy until the consecration. I would constantly be under surveillance. I was to wear a bullet-proof vest unless I was in a bullet-proof car they would provide.

He again introduced Miss Kennedy. He assured me that Ms. Kennedy did have a Ph.D. in biochemistry and had been working for them since the age of fifteen. I reminded him of the child labor laws and that I wasn't interested in knowing the details of her life. My own life was boring enough; she smiled. She probably had the same training he had. I asked about the Pope, and he assured me that the Pope was healthy and safe. I asked how they could protect the Pope during his worldwide travels. He said that they couldn't. That surprised me, but his next announcement didn't. The Pope would remain in the Vatican until his trip to Moscow. "You arrested the Pope?" I asked. They had explained the situation to His Holiness, and since he was a lot smarter than I was, it was his decision to remain in the Vatican. Besides, we were talking about a period of a few months, provided the church in Barcelona was completed soon.

He told me that I had the following choices: I could be in solitary confinement in prison after some cocaine was planted on me; I could join a monastery that they secured, or I could cooperate with them. He assured me that Miss Kennedy was my type. They had decided what type of person I would be most attracted to. I told them that Miss Kennedy was every man's type and that these comments were the most ridiculous of the night. No, he suggested that while every man would love to be with Miss Kennedy, some might prefer a woman who was an inch taller or shorter, some might prefer a woman with a different hair color or eye color, and that she was guaranteed to be my absolute ideal. I thanked him for his analysis and asked Ms. Kennedy how she felt about being described in those terms. She smiled that training smile and said that she was flattered.

I told him that until my trip to Rome next week, I would start in the monastery. He said that would be fine. He mentioned that whatever choice I selected that it would be important to get along with Miss Kennedy because she would always be with me whenever I was in public. I asked why she would be better than the gorilla who moved into the apartment next to me. He smiled again and said that Miss Kennedy was an expert in martial arts and would be more effective because, as a woman, she could walk closer to me. She could hold my hand, put her arm around me, and pull me out of danger faster.

He again asked why I was being so difficult about all this and complimented me for being much smarter than I appeared. I told him that the years of suffering, starving, living in the desert, and looking for work made me value my recently won freedom. Freedom was more important than extreme wealth, and it was the freedom that they were taking away.

CHAPTER 44

THE MONASTERY

THE NEXT DAY I was taken to a Trappist Monk Monastery in upstate New York. The monks get up in the middle of the night to pray. They pray throughout the day and night like Moslems, who pray five times a day. They are devoted to prayer and to progressing in the spiritual life. While frequently criticized because of their departure from actively solving the world's problems, they continue the spiritual battle to save the world. We can not defeat the Evil One except by grace and by progressing in the spiritual life. On the other hand, we can not improve the suffering in the world by being locked in a cell. God and the Evil One act directly and indirectly. Man must do the same. He must do all he can to help his neighbor by the physical means at his disposal, do something directly, and by his prayers indirectly. The cloistered societies of monks and nuns emphasize the indirect form of help. Make no mistake about it; prayers are powerful. Just ask Father Dayton, Father Benjamin, and Mr. Tandler.

The monastery was on a hill surrounded by a vast forest. The lawns were immolated. There was a small gift shop near the entrance where the hospitality monk would sell religious items and the jam preservatives that the monks manufactured. They also made the clothing that the priests wore during the celebration of the mass.

The monks also ran a retreat house. Visitors could walk through the grounds, use the retreat house and attend Mass. They could listen to the prayers through the glass enclosure but could not receive communion. Neither the monks nor the visitors could see each other. The visitors could hear the monks, but the monks could not hear the visitors. It was an elaborate setup. The rest of the building where the monks ate, slept, and worked were off-limits to the public. They could not be seen by the visitors.

By withdrawing from the world and with simple manual labor, the monk was to have the time to advance in the spiritual life. I would be cloistered from the public but was not required to participate in any of the activities of daily work or prayer. I was free to remain in solitary confinement. There were fifty-four monks living in the community. Except for the few working in the gift shop and retreat house, all were cloistered from the public.

I was brought to a simple cell. It contained a small desk, a bed, a dresser, a lamp, and copious reading material. I remained in the monastery for about a week. It reminded me of my years in the Arabian desert. The around-the-clock calls for prayer, the isolation, and the loneliness brought back memories of those painful times. I could enjoy the walks in the forest. It was much better than the desert, but what I longed for was freedom. The monastery cured me of my "attitude" problems. From now on, I would take the money and the security and cooperate with the CIA. The monastery was better than the prison but very similar.

CHAPTER 45

MS. KENNEDY

I WAS TO MEET Cardinal O'Connor, Cardinal Law, Pope John Paul II, and several other officials at the Vatican.

Travel on commercial airlines was less conspicuous than using chartered flights. I had a window seat in first class. Sitting next to me was the ever-present Ms. Kennedy, "my wife."

She told me what clothes to wear, informed me how I was expected to behave at the Vatican, and reminded me of the security measures that had been worked out. I could go anywhere in the world at the expense of the CIA; I only had to remain with Miss Kennedy twenty-four hours a day and make sure that the CIA was always informed of my travel plans. I could use the men's room in our hotel room. Every other men's room was off-limits. I was never to leave Miss Kennedy when in public. I had to wear a vest and other security equipment. All conversations in public were recorded. There would always be undercover people accompanying us. Also, at any hotel I chose from Ms. Kennedy's list, agents would occupy the remaining rooms on the floor.

Ms. Kennedy was a very unusual person. She was the author of several books via a pseudo name, traveled throughout the world, spoke Russian, German, French, Spanish, and Italian and had participated in several marathon races, and was a world-class skier. I was a gorilla, Neanderthal, who she had to keep out of trouble. When I asked why she was telling me all of this, she answered that I was her last assignment. Her ten years were over, so it was time to retire. I asked if we might go to Munich and to Medjugorje and was told that they had anticipated this request. Arrangements to go to Munich were already made, and she was brushing up on her Croatian. At this point, nothing surprised me. I asked if she minded being temporarily rejected in favor of the monastery and was told that there were no hard feelings because if a complete idiot had made the wrong choice, why should she care? She didn't feel rejected by someone who preferred to be isolated from God. She didn't believe in god and thought that I was psychotic.

With my diplomatic passport in hand, we walked to the waiting automobile and checked into the hotel. There was one queen-sized bed in the room. I knew that Ms. Kennedy was employed by the CIA. The next question was whether she was also being used by the Evil One. Since October 15, 1982, I had been celibate and hoped that in spite of my human frailties, that would not change until I was married. Ms. Kennedy had already demonstrated her superior intellect and her superiority in most other aspects of life. To her, I was an ugly, rude, unkept gorilla humanoid who was part of the animal world. I was her last assignment, an ugly pet thrust upon her by some superstitious nonsense. There was no God, and if there was a God, he had the extremely poor taste to pick a sub-human like me. She had seen the tapes of the healing of Mr. Tandler but thought it was in the realm of statistical possibility. There are known cases of spontaneous regression of tumors. I had been in the right place at the right time to take advantage of this phenomenon. She had not heard of the healings of Father Dayton or of Father Benjamin, but they probably would not have opened her otherwise perfect mind.

At first, we were both very suspicious of each other. I thought she was there to do her job for the CIA and to do her job to keep me from heaven. She "knew" that although I pretended to believe in this non-existent God and belonged to the sub-homo sapiens class, it was only a matter of time before I would make the usual physical advances.

She hoped that I would accept her rejection gracefully without her having to hurt me physically. Until that point was reached when I would succumb to her charms and be rejected, the relationship would never be stabilized and finalized. Of course, I was attracted to her. The fifty-four monks would have been attracted to her. It was too bad we couldn't have met under more normal circumstances. Then, I probably would have broken my back to get her to turn her head and notice me. Then again, if I wasn't forced upon her by these unusual circumstances, she would have noticed me as someone who had just stepped in the wrong place and was attempting to clean her shoe. I would have appeared as a foul-smelling accident that had to be wiped away.

We checked into our suite with the queen-sized bed. I proceeded with my few belongings, and I could sense the increased tension in Ms. Kennedy. It was bad enough that she had to sit next to me on the airplane, but even her superhuman tolerance was being tested by my sloppiness and the thought that she would have to share the same bathroom with this animal. How would you like to share toilet facilities with a cat or dog? I mean to have the dog or cat physically sit on the same toilet seat you were using. That was what was going through her mind. It didn't help matters that I was sloppy. I never flossed my yellow teeth, and I didn't care what kind of food I put in my mouth as long as the food didn't immediately get me sick. I knew the relationship between fats and cardiovascular disease but was more interested in my cheeseburgers than in prolonging my life for a few years. Ms. Kennedy, schedule permitting, would shower twice a day, brush her teeth after every meal or snack, would not subject herself to fats, grease, or preservatives, flossed her white teeth daily, and was meticulously neat. Now while on this job, she had to loosen up. Her photographic memory allowed her to notice the least change in the arrangement of anything in the room. It angered her if I moved something just before we left the room. She was trying to get through her last assignment. Hopefully, the church in Barcelona will be finished in a couple of months, and then the consecration will take place on November 7. Then her assignment would be completed, and she would retire.

CHAPTER 46

THE VATICAN

I WAS BROUGHT TO the Vatican by Cardinal Law and Cardinal O'Connor. Ms. Kennedy remained in the hotel.

There had been a meeting the day before between the two cardinals, the Pope, Cardinal Ratzinger, and Cardinal Casarelli, the Vatican Secretary of State. Everything had been discussed without me, but his holiness the Pope had decided to withhold his decision until he met me. I was asked if I was ready to pray for someone ill because it would probably be necessary. The CIA had found a blind priest who the Pope and his two most powerful Cardinals, Ratzinger, and Casarelli) knew personally. The stage was set. The performance would begin momentarily.

"As Jesus was walking along, he saw a man who had been born blind. His disciples asked him, 'Teacher, whose sin caused him to be born blind? Was it his own or his parent's sin?' Jesus answered, 'Hi, blindness has nothing to do with his sins or his parent's sins. He is blind so that God's power might be seen at work in him....'

After he said this, Jesus spat on the ground and made some mud with his spittle; he rubbed the mud on the man's eyes and told him, 'G and wash your face in the Pool of Siloam' (This meant 'sent'). So the man went, washed his face, and came back seeing....

Then they took to the Pharisees the man who had been blind. The day that Jesus made the mud and cured his blindness was a Sabbath. The Pharisees then asked the man again how he had received his sight. He told them, 'He put some mud on my eyes, I washed my face, and now I can see.'

Some of the Pharisees said, 'The man who did this can not be from God, for he does not obey the Sabbath law.'

Others, however, said, 'how could a man who is a sinner perform such miracles as these?' And there was a division among them. So the Pharisees asked the man once more, 'You say he cured you of your blindness – well, what do you say about him?'

'He is a prophet,' the man answered.

The Jewish authorities, however, were not willing to believe that he had been blind and could now see until they called his parents.

A second time they called back the man who had been born blind and said to him, 'Promise before God that you will tell the truth. We know that this man who cured you is a sinner.'

'I do not know if he is a sinner or not,' the man replied. 'One thing I do know: I was blind, and now I can see.'…

'Since the beginning of the world, nobody has ever heard of anyone giving sight to a person born blind. Unless this man came from God, he would not be able to do such a thing.'

'They answered, 'You were born blind' And you are trying to teach us? And they expelled him from the synagogue." (John 9:1-3, 13-18, 24-28, 32-34).

I was brought before the four Cardinals and his holiness Pope John Paul II. The Pope had that smile, that way about him, that magnetism or charisma that people talk about, and instantly you knew you were in the presence of a great man. He had his special vestments on and was probably about to conduct a service. Each Pope picks his own emblem to place on his vestments: On one side near his right shoulder was the Blessed Virgen Mary, and near the other shoulder was a picture of St. Peter and St. Paul. I was with the most important Pope since Peter. I asked for the blessing of the four cardinals and the Holy Father.

Then the blind priest was brought in. He was a small man, about five feet tall and seventy years old. He had been blind from glaucoma for about twenty-five years and lived in a nearby monastery. I began with the rosary, read the bible, prayed the stations of the cross, and anointed the priest. Immediately he could see! The old priest started jabbering in Italian. Previously I was speaking English, and except for the priest, everyone could understand. It didn't matter. All that mattered was the priest's happiness and the smile on the Pope's face.

The Pope pulled me aside and said that we would meet next week in Moscow. He told me that it was necessary for him to see this because he now had to cancel several trips until the consecration. He was the great shepherd. He wanted to see his flock and spread the word. Being confined to the Vatican would not be easy. He told me that the architects had already begun the work on the Church of the Holy Family in Barcelona and that it was long overdue. He put his hand on my forehead and prayed for me. We embraced, and as tears ran down my cheeks, I heard him ask me to pray for him every day until the consecration.

CHAPTER 47

RETURN TO MUNICH

BACK AT THE HOTEL, Ms. Kennedy brought me back to earth. She asked about the "miracle thing" and asked me, as a "Man of God," if I could please remember to pick up my socks and underwear. We were scheduled to fly to Munich that day.

When we arrived in Munich, we checked into the Four Seasons Hotel. I told her I would be happy to show her the dining room because I was at this hotel previously. I didn't stay at the hotel but did eat at the restaurant. The food was great! She had been to this hotel and restaurant many times and was amazed at my enthusiasm. She pretended that she was never there previously until the maître-D (a different one from October 15, 1982) recognized her and spoiled her little game. The piano player was different from the one I remembered. The food was also different. It was very, very good, but on October 15, 1982, I had been invited by a very special host, and He wasn't as evident today. Your company at the table influences your enjoyment of the meal, and Ms. Kennedy has a lot to learn from Jesus.

The next day we set out for Tears Church and Neuschwanstein Castle, but I wanted to first stop at the bakery near the Marienplatz, the main square near the city hall building. It was just a few blocks away, and we were going to bring some of the bread back to our hotel room. As we were waiting in line, Ms. Kennedy suddenly pushed me over the table where the daily bread was placed. I didn't know that she was the one who pushed me. All I realized was that I was in a pile of bread, blood was coming down my eye, and people were screaming in German. A wild-looking man with dark skin was wielding a knife. He was about to stab Ms. Kennedy. I jumped out of the pile of bread, bumped into the back and shoulder of Ms. Kennedy, and attempted to grab the man with the knife before he stabbed her. The man was sent flying. He stumbled out the door and disappeared into the crowd. We went back to the hotel room, where Ms. Kennedy started screaming at me. She was out of control. She couldn't believe how stupid I was. What more could she do? She saw this peculiar-looking man about to take out his knife. She threw me out of the way and positioned herself between the man and me. Her back was to me so she could see the man at all times. He had stolen some bread and was leaving. She moved to let him pass. All of a sudden, I decided to jump out of safety to stop this man who was on his way out of the store with a couple of loaves of bread. I pushed into her and was trying to get stabbed by this poor robber. There was no greater sin, according to Ms. Kennedy than stupidity. She stopped screaming when she noticed some blood on my shirt near my belt.

I had blood on my shirt from some of the abrasions on my eyebrow and chin. But now we both realized that I had been stabbed in the side of my chest where the vest didn't protect me. It was a very, very superficial skin wound. The knife had scratched the surface of the skin. I was fine. However, if I wanted to maintain the little freedom that I had, this was a disaster that had to be acted upon immediately. It was alright for me to be bleeding from minor abrasions sustained at the hands of Ms. Kennedy, but to be bleeding from a knife wound was a failure of the security system. I was very sore over the area. The shirt I was wearing had to be destroyed before the rest of the security forces saw what had happened. Obviously, I didn't want to be examined by a physician. I didn't need much medical care, just a bandage, and a topical antibiotic.

Ms. Kennedy was also hopeful that the wound could be concealed. She didn't want to finish her illustrious career as a failure because some ignoramus lost control of his senses and jumped out from a position of safety.

I jumped into the shower while Ms. Kennedy used the phone. She told them that I was fine but would need a couple of bandages, peroxide, and a local antibiotic ointment to clean my head abrasions. After I got out of the shower, I spoke to someone on the phone and told them that I was fine. I just pulled a couple of muscles and preferred to rest in the hotel room for the rest of the day. There was no reason to suspect anything. I did walk back to the hotel room and appeared fine after leaving the bakery.

I was not lying when I said that I had pulled some muscles. From being thrown over the table, I was sore and had difficulty walking. There was no major injury, but I could not walk with my usual gait. This was a catastrophe. I didn't want to be examined. We needed time. I may have been over six feet two inches tall and almost two hundred pounds, but I was out of condition. I was a wimp, limping around the room. After a couple of hours, Ms. Kennedy's anger started to subside. Slowly it started to sink in that I had jumped at the robber because, from my view, it appeared that he was about to stab her. It was like watching a dog throw himself in front of a car in an attempt to stop the car from running over a child. Even though the dog is not human, you marvel at his courage and loyalty. I was a sub-human to Ms. Kennedy, so the analogy fit. I tried to explain that I wasn't thinking of myself. I wasn't thinking at all, just reacting. She asked how I could be so stupid. Didn't I realize that she had everything under control? Didn't I realize that she would always have everything under control as long as I followed her instructions?.

After this episode in the bakery, things were different. I was no longer a sub-human but instead a stupid child, but at least I was now human. Ms. Kennedy became Marybeth. We still had the problem of what to do if I was limping around the next day, but for now, everything was fine. We ordered room service and washed the blood out of my shirt with peroxide. Then I went to sleep.

After a short nap, I started to read and then think about the recent events. I was lying in the room in my new CIA-acquired expensive pajamas; previously, I always went to bed in my underwear. Why did I try to save Marybeth? I didn't even like her. Yes, she was physically attractive and brilliant, but she always ridiculed me. She always made me feel like I was in a lower class (which I was). Even when she wasn't putting me down, her usual behavior and manner brought forth my contrasting ineptitude and clumsiness. When you are near someone who is beautiful, your lack of beauty is more evident. When I'm in the presence of a saintly man, it's so easy for me to realize that I'm a sinner. I could not imagine the filth that comes out of my mind being present in his. God, I never claimed to be intelligent, but was it necessary that I be around someone who wrote books, spoke so many languages, and had a photographic memory? Anyway, who cares how smart she is? Who cares about the games she plays pretending to be ignorant?

CHAPTER 48

———

BARCELONA, SPAIN

THE NEXT MORNING I felt worse. It was difficult to straighten up, let alone walk normally. We procrastinated. I told Marybeth that I couldn't do it. I told her that the only out of this mess was to tell them that we were staying in the hotel room again. Tell them that we were rolling around in bed. Tell them anything. She burst out laughing and said that they would never believe her. They knew that she would no sooner have anything to do with me than with a goat.

I told her to have faith. After all of the miracles that they had heard or seen (actually videotaped), they might think it was another miracle of sorts. She then asked how I could do such a disgusting thing if I was a man of God performing miracles. I said that it was easy to explain. I wasn't performing miracles; God was. Hadn't she heard about David and Solomon? David decided to have Bathsheba for his wife. First, he was guilty of adultery, and then he had her husband murdered. Solomon, the wise, his son by Bathsheba, ended his life marrying many foreign, non-Jewish women and encouraging the worship of their gods. People who were chosen by God have their moments of failure like everyone else. Hopefully, they repent and start again. It was more plausible for me to fall from grace because of the perfect woman than for her to fall from grace because of me.

Let's face it; there was no alternative. I couldn't leave the room. They would examine me and place me under house arrest. What else can a man and woman be doing in s hotel room for the whole day? She asked with a smile; how could I be expected to last the entire day in my pathetic physical condition? I told her that I must have done a lot of sleeping before and after. She made the call. They were skeptical but confessed that the supernatural was unpredictable. They bought it. I was happy. She was very insulted. She was also bored to death being locked up in a room with me all day. She said that the only thing I knew anything about was the bible, which she had read and memorized. So we talked about the bible for a while, and I went back to sleep. Marybeth hardly ever slept. Three or four hours a night was sufficient for her, so she was used to being in a room with me while I slept. It was more difficult for her to be in a room with me when I was awake.

The next morning I felt a lot better. I was still a little stiff, but that could now be explained by the acrobatics in the hotel room. I rolled over to take a short nap after breakfast (room service). I was very tired. I guess the stress of the episode in the bakery was still present. Marybeth woke me up and said that we had to go to Barcelona. We had to go because there was a major snag in completing the Church of the Sacred Family. If it was not completed within a few months, we would have to wait until November 7 of the following year. That might be too late. We had to leave immediately.

We arrived at the Cardinal's residence in time for the meeting with the architect, several engineers, the leader of a civic group, the mayor, and a Vatican representative. The Cardinal greeted Marybeth (my translator) and me. He was very appreciative that my company from America would pay the expenses for such a national project. The late Antonio Gaudi, the famous Spanish architect who started construction in 1884, had left plans for how the construction was to be completed. He was religious and left his heart in the work of the cathedral. It was sacrilegious to even consider using alternate plans to finish the construction. There was no amount of money, financial pressure, or physical coercion that could change this. The reason it had taken so long to complete the church was because the remaining work was very expensive and time-consuming because of the nature of Gaudi's unique architectural design. The project was doomed to remain unfinished for decades. At this point, there were private buildings that were built on adjoining land that had to be demolished to make room for the completed church. The request to have the church completed was not a simple one. I remember seeing a picture of Gaudi marching in a Corpus Christi (Body of Christ) parade. He was a national hero then. Now that he was dead, he was even more of a hero. It was impossible to alter his plans now; it would be similar to altering Michaelangelo's plans for a partially completed project. None of the people in the room knew about the Pope's consecration except Marybeth and me.

I started my address to this group with comments about the unique architectural style of the cathedral. The wishes of Gaudi must be followed so that the completed cathedral would remain unique. I told them that my company would continue to support the construction with as much money and for as much time as was needed. This brought a warm round of applause from everyone in the room except the Vatican representative, who brought a message from the Pope that the church was to be completed within a couple of months. I also said that my company had no desire to do anything that would displease the Holy Father. The fundamental purpose of any church was to distribute the Body and Blood of Jesus to the faithful. In order to function, the church must have a roof and completed walls. My plan was a two-phased approach. Get any type of construction started to complete the walls and roof within a couple of months and start daily Mass. At the same time, money would be placed in a special account. This would placate the country which would be outraged because it would appear that Gaudi's plans were temporarily being pushed aside. This temporary period could end up being twenty or thirty years. The account would help alleviate the anxiety because the Spanish public could inspect the account and see that, ultimately, all of Gaudi's wishes would be followed. Then there was a general discussion about how this was a noble plan that was doomed to failure because of countless public protests that would halt construction as soon as the public realized that Gaudi's wishes were even temporarily ignored. I could now understand the urgent call from the CIA. There was no amount of force that could change the views of so many people. It wasn't about altering the opinions of the people in the room; the entire Spanish population would be in an uproar! A dead man's wishes could not be altered, and every society had a certain respect for the dead. Spain wasn't unique in this regard. It suddenly dawned on me that there was only one course to follow:

> "Jesus went to a town named Nain, accompanied by his disciples and a large crowd. Just as he arrived at the gate of the town, a funeral procession was coming out. The dead man was the only son of a woman who was a widow, and a large crowd from the town was with her. When the Lord saw her, his heart was filled with pity for her, and he said to her, 'Don't cry.' Then he walked over and touched the coffin, and the men carrying it stopped. Jesus said, 'Young man. Get up, I tell you.' The dead man sat up and began to talk, and Jesus gave him back to his mother. They were all filled with fear and praised God. 'A great prophet has appeared among us,' they said. 'god has come to save his people." (Luke 7:11-16).

As someone was contacting the physician, I pulled the Cardinal aside and told him that if he was open to the Holy Spirit, he would be given a sign from God to follow my plans. I asked him to call the nearby cemeteries to determine if anyone was about to be buried. He thought it was an odd request but was grateful for my financial aid. He was still hopeful to see the cathedral completed before he died.

Two hours later, a group of mourners was surprised to see the Cardinal and our little group descend upon them at the cemetery. The priest was shocked to see the Cardinal. A widow was standing at the grave site of her son, her only child. The dead man was thirty-four years old and had died suddenly in an automobile accident. As I started to pray, I asked the Cardinal to order the cemetery attendant to lift the cover of the coffin so that the physician could superficially examine the prospective patient (no pulse, no respirations, pupils unresponsive to light and dilated – the pupils were fixed and dilated). The crowd was motionless and watched all of this, too stunned to protest. The Cardinal was universally respected for anyone to protest that the body was being desecrated. Marybeth continued to translate while I was praying. I finished my prayers by anointing the dead man's forehead. This was strictly forbidden by the church. The oil for anointing the sick could not be used on the dead. I finished making the sign of the cross with the oil, and he started to move. HE WAS ALIVE! Several people fainted. Marybeth was pale and couldn't translate anymore. I shook her and told her that this was the moment I needed her most of all. I embraced the mother and son and then told them and the crowd via Marybeth, "It was the wish of our Immaculate Mother in heaven, the Blessed Virgin Mary, that the previous dead man is the first to receive communion in the completed Church of the Sacred Family within two months."

All of the people from our meeting were there. The debate was over. Marybeth and I were out of the country within forty-five minutes. As we boarded our private jet, I could see that Marybeth was still astonished. The raising of the dead was not a mathematical possibility. There were cases where patients dropped their blood pressure and stopped breathing and then were immediately resuscitated, but never was a corpse brought back to life except in the bible. Not only was she astonished to discover that God existed and proved His presence to her by this resurrection, but also because He had decided to pick me as His instrument. Meanwhile, I was praying to God to forgive me for putting words in the mouth of the Blessed Virgin Mary. Who was I to tell the crowd of this nonsense of her nonexistent requests? It is precisely because of the possibility that a visionary might mislead the public that the church must take its time in evaluating reports of the appearance of Mary and other supernatural events. I hoped God would understand the motive and forgive the action.

CHAPTER 49

A VISIT TO MEDJUGORJE, YUGOSLAVIA

To Marybeth, I was now James. I was a person at last. She was following her orders and doing her job protecting me. Before, she did not believe in God, nor did she believe that if I was not present at the consecration, a nuclear war would result. She asked how the nuclear war would start, and I told her that bombs would be set off by themselves. The Evil One would do that. Every nuclear missile in the world is launched or explodes in place. She started talking about codes and computers, and I told her that although I didn't know much about computers, I had already seen a demonstration of supernatural computer functions. The computer would be infected with a virus, and the nuclear weapons would have a combination of some being launched and some exploding in place. She was shocked by all of this. So was I. I then told her to forget what I had just said. But she persisted in questioning me. I told her that it was perfectly logical for the Evil One to use whatever method of destruction was available. Man built the weapons. The Evil One would now use man's creation to annihilate the human race.

When she realized that the entire planet would have been destroyed if that robber had stabbed me to death, she started to scream at me again! This was worse than the first time. How could I do something so stupid? Where was my sense of responsibility? Before, she was screaming at me because my ineptitude had prevented her from doing her job with the utmost efficiency. That was bad enough. This screaming was so much worse. The veins in her neck looked like they were about to burst. I didn't try to defend myself this time; I wasn't thinking but reacting instinctively to the situation. I simply told her the truth. It was her fault! I was in love with her. I asked if her verbal assault could be toned down until after the consecration. Then she would never have to see me again. She was moved. Tears started streaming from her blue eyes. Her lips started quivering. She was speechless. I was a dog who had thrown himself in front of the oncoming car to save the child. Except now I was a human being, not just a messy assignment.

After we returned to the Four Seasons hotel in Munich, she received a phone call from her boss. He said that despite all of the publicity that the picture of the son standing there waving his death certificate would generate, things would die down soon. They were working on limiting the reports of this episode to Spain, where it would work to the benefit of early completion of the church. In the future, would we be so kind as to inform him that a major damage control operation might be necessary? He didn't know what we were up to until we arrived at the cemetery. A little warning would have helped. There was only a general description of me – tall, with dark hair, and spoke English. Marybeth was identified as the beautiful translator. We would receive new passports and identification papers tomorrow. We were given permission to visit Medjugorje, but then we had to return home.

Marybeth and I visited all of the places in Munich that were important to me. We went to Tears Church, Neuschwanstein Castle, the Residence, Frauenkirche, and the Wittlesbach Fountain. Then we traveled to Medjugorje. We stayed in the nearby city of Mostar. We arrived at St. James Church in time for morning prayers, walked and prayed the stations of the cross, and visited the huge cross on the hill. Marybeth was one of a handful of people selected from the vast crowd to enter the small room where the Blessed Virgin Mary would visit the visionaries. This was nothing unusual for Marybeth. She was always picked out of a crowd. She tried to get me to come with her, but I wasn't selected, and the priest would not let me enter. I looked like all the other people in the crowd. How could she leave me alone unguarded? If anything happened to me while she was in the apparition room, most of the people on the planet would die. I told her that I would be safe in the church, that this was a once-in-a-lifetime invitation for her, and that despite the fact that it was illogical and stupid to leave me that she should try it once. Stupidity and nonsense have a rightful place also. I told her that it was really illogical for her to believe that she could protect me from the Evil One; only God could do that. All He asks is that we do our best. The rest is up to Him. I would be safe for a couple of minutes in His house.

She went into the apparition room and found me in the church twenty minutes later. The people in our accompanying surveillance team did not report that we were apart for twenty minutes. The CIA was malfunctioning at its highest level, but the world continued to revolve on its axis. It was dark by the time the long church service was over.

On the way back to Mostar, she told me of the faces of the two visionaries who were talking to Mary. No one else could see Mary or hear her. Then the visionaries told the people about Mary's message that day. Mary was leading us to the forgiveness of God. We should submit ourselves to His will. God understands the intentions of every heart. Convert. Say the Rosary and make use of all of the sacraments. This was one of the few times I could imagine when it helped to be able to speak Croatian. Marybeth was invited to the home of one of the visionaries the next day. As usual, she was an instant sensation. How many people in the world looked like Marybeth and spoke Croatian? She was unique; she was the Babe Ruth of the Medjugorje pilgrims!

The next day we went to the visionary's simple home. I felt uneasy lying, saying that Marybeth and I were married. Also, I could sense the disappointment in everyone's eyes when I was introduced. How could Marybeth be married to someone who looked like me? Ok, so I wasn't a movie star. Is that such a crime? From the appearance of everyone in the room except Marybeth, God wasn't so concerned with her comely appearance. There were noses as big as mine and other features as coarse as mine everywhere in the village. The visionary was happy to talk to Marybeth. No interpreter was needed. Marybeth was so intelligent, and people were always drawn to her. I had no idea what anyone was saying. Periodically Marybeth would translate a few words into English, or one of the other people in the room would attempt to say something in broken English. Otherwise, I was alone in a crowded room for about two hours. As we left, the visionary and some members of her family gave us warm goodbyes and commented on how impressed they were with Marybeth's faith. They told me that I was lucky to have Marybeth.

These last comments did it. I was fuming! In her usual perfect performance, Marybeth had used her training and her personal charm to mislead these people. I believed in God, not Marybeth! I wasn't lucky to have Marybeth. I wasn't her husband. What was going on here? It was time to go home. I had seen enough of Medjugorje yesterday. So we headed back to the hotel in Mostar.

On the way back to the hotel, I told Marybeth my thoughts. I edited some of them. She said that she did not mislead them and that she did believe in God. If these people were impressed with her faith, it was because she was not lying and putting on a performance. Since that dead man got out of the coffin, she believed! I asked her how she knew that the man was really dead. Maybe it was an elaborate setup. She had seen the man's non-reactive, dilated pupils for herself. She listed the few drugs that could cause dilated pupils. With each drug, the dose necessary to cause that effect would also cause the patient to be on intravenous medication and a ventilator to support life. So she knew more about medicine than I did. So what! Who cares how much information she knows? I was even more angry. I stopped pouting as we entered our hotel room.

The phone rang. It was the boss. Instead of going home, we were scheduled to fly to Moscow the next day. President Gorbachev wanted to see me. I told her to get back on the phone, call her boss and tell him that I wasn't going! I wanted to go home. I wanted to be in my tiny apartment. I wanted to go to a Red Sox game.

She looked at me in complete astonishment. What was I saying? Just when she started to believe that I was a human being, a sane one at that, I was talking such gibberish. Haven't I learned anything at all? You don't say no to her boss. Did I want to end up in prison? You won't disappoint the KGB. Obviously, they were following us in Barcelona and had seen the dead man get out of the coffin. When President Gorbachev says that he wants to see you and is told that the KGB and CIA are taking care of it, he expects to see you. For years the KGB and CIA had been competing in every part of the world, and now they were working together on this consecration. Didn't I know that on the same day that I was stabbed, President Bush had met with President Gorbachev? She knew that I was upset and pouting, but let's get on with it. This is a big time. You have a responsibility to go to Moscow, and besides, you have enough problems to solve without becoming emotionally involved with the Red Sox.

Did I really say that I wanted to go to a Red Sox game? I sat down, took a few breaths, and found some bottled water to drink. I recalled the many times that I had questioned my own sanity. This was too much for me. I told her that I was going to bed and would discuss the matter in the morning. I needed some rest. This day was bad enough. Now it's time to go to sleep. Tomorrow I'll look at this again.

I got up the next morning and realized that I didn't have a choice. We were going to Moscow. I was speaking to the boss on the phone. Previously he would only speak to Marybeth. He was desperate! Didn't I realize how many starving people could be fed with the millions of dollars that the CIA was giving me? He told me that I was a very wealthy man who had a large stake in keeping this planet from exploding. He asked me if I would like the shipments of food and clothing to Africa to begin immediately. There were warring factions in East Africa that were causing the starvation of millions. He continued to offer me everything and anything that the

CIA and KGB could provide. From the sound of his voice, I could tell he was no longer smiling. He was afraid to coerce me because I seemed on the verge of cracking up. He was very frustrated.

I told him that I expected the war in Africa to stop and that the food should be delivered immediately. If the CIA and KGB can't take care of this little mess in Africa, how could they be trusted to put on the consecration? He sounded like he was choking. He paused and then assured me that it would be done as soon as I stepped on the chartered plane to Moscow. Then he quietly asked to speak to Marybeth. Marybeth picked up the receiver and got blasted for not doing a better job controlling me. He was glad that she was retiring because, obviously, she had lost it. She assured him that I would be on the plane shortly with the proper attitude.

I expected her to hang up the phone and start screaming at me again. Instead, she was very quiet. She realized that my comment about wanting to see a Red Sox game indicated that I was unraveling before her eyes. Her job was to patch things up as best she could until the consecration. She detested the Red Sox; they were a professional band of three stooges who were hopeless. She wasn't a sports fan. There was no sense in rooting for a team unless you were the owner, coach, general manager, or player of the team. However, she was well acquainted with the curse of the Bambino, though until recently, she did not believe in God. Even people who deny God realize that the Red Sox are cursed.

She turned towards me and, in a very soft voice, asked if I would like them to buy Red Sox for me. I said, "That would be fine, but only if they destroy Fenway Park and move the team to Rhode Island. She said that could be arranged. Anything I wanted could be arranged if I could just pull myself together and cooperate. Didn't I realize that we were all on the same side? She helped me pack my clothes. She said that although I had acted in a very immature fashion yesterday, I was forgiven.

"Be a man," she said. "You look like a man. You're over six feet two inches tall and have hair on your chest, so act like one."

So that is why I had grown an inch in height and started to grow hair on my chest. So this robot of an excuse of a person would think that I looked like a man. My blood pressure shot up, but I didn't say anything. We both slowly walked around the room and quietly prepared to leave. We didn't want to blow the last fuse that was keeping me together.

CHAPTER 50

—⌣⫘⌣—

MOSCOW, THE CAPITAL OF THE GENTILE WORLD

THE SOVIET UNION WAS the most amazing country that ever existed. With the Russian Revolution of 1917, it was founded on the old tried and true method of force, coercion, and murder. That's not what made it amazing. It was the ideology, the Marxist-Leninism, the planned central control of the economy, the manipulation of the price and services, and the capitalist-proletariat literature that went with the tyranny that made Russia different. The Russians were forced to learn all of this philosophy and live it. Of Course, Hitler and Stalin could sign a non-aggression pact and divide up Poland. Except for this economic mumbo jumbo (for it was voodoo economics), Hitler and Stalin were identical. It took about seventy years for these advanced thinkers to suddenly realize that this economic system does not work. One day a little old man got on the loudspeaker and, like the Emperor's New Cloths, announced to the bewildered crowd that Communism doesn't work. You can not manipulate prices and pretend that a rare item in great demand can be maintained at a low price indefinitely. A country with vast oil and mineral wealth, with institutions of higher education that enabled the Soviet union to built the first nuclear reactor, put the first Sputnik into orbit, and put the first man in space was reduced to not being able to provide food, housing or basic consumer items to a large part of their working population. Unless you were privileged, you stood in endless lines for non-existent consumer items.

Fortunately, there are no more Communists in the Soviet Union, just as there are not any Nazis in Germany. This atheist, communist philosophy was foreign to the average Russian. It had to be rammed down his throat through torture and mass extermination. At one point, one-third of the population of Leningrad had been imprisoned or detained. Mr. Gorbachev was trying to change all of this.

I arrived at the Kremlin, a fortress of government buildings, the previous residence of the Czars (Russian for Caesar). St. Paul would have been proud of me. Marybeth and I joined Gorbachev, Foreign Minister Eduard Shevardnadze, a KGB official, a General, U.S. Secretary of State James Baker, and someone from the CIA who I had not previously met. Gorbachev embraced Marybeth and said it was good to see her again and that the pictures from Spain did not do her justice. Marybeth knew everyone! She could walk into the North Pole observatory and, within two minutes, find someone she had met years ago. As they were chatting, she nodded to some of the other Soviet officials, who smiled at her and welcomed her to their side. Then the meeting turned towards me. I was not part of this well-known club, so the vocabulary dropped to the elementary school level.

Mr. Gorbachev outlined his plans. He wanted to see me perform another miracle. He would let all of the bishops in the world and the Pope come to Moscow and consecrate Russia to the Immaculate Heart of Mary on November 7. He would do this out of respect for the Vatican and for President Bush. He said that after seeing the films of the episode in Barcelona and the video of Mr. Tandler and reading the CIA reports of the other healings, he was alarmed that perhaps the world would be destroyed if the consecration was not carried out. So he had decided to not only cooperate indirectly but to take an active part in the consecration. It was to be his project. He would ensure safety and provide travel and housing arrangements for all of the bishops and the Pope. It would be done at Russian expense and under Russian supervision. He had already given his word to President Bush and Pope John Paul II that they could count on him to overcome any problem. Great, so what was the purpose of this meeting? Why was I here? Why did I have to perform again?

Now came the deal. Gorbachev and the Russian leadership, in the true spirit of comradeship, had decided to capitalize on the consecration in the true sense of the word economically. They had the Pope, the bishops, the icon, the church, and now the CIA had promised to deliver me, the miracle worker, so they were all set. They envisioned a several-month emergency plan similar to the previous five-year economic plans to construct an adjoining city next to Moscow. The city would provide accommodations for an estimated fifteen million pilgrims a year. This investment was to start as soon as we reached an understanding at this meeting. The Cathedral would be filled to capacity with all of the bishops and religious officials. Political leaders would fill the surrounding area within the Kremlin, and the Red Square would be filled with a collection of sick people from around the world. On that day, the consecration would be accompanied by the miraculous healing of thousands who would return home cured. Then Moscow would be a combination of Lourdes/Fatima/Rome of the world. The economic future would be stabilized by the influx of hard currency. Gorbachev stated that on that day, he would be the first Soviet-era President to begin daily church worship. He asked for my thoughts and, more importantly, my cooperation. He wanted to see me in action and had a list of patients who could be brought in immediately. He wanted to make sure that I was the real thing he had read about in the bible. He also wanted to see me cure more than one person at a time. His grand plan wouldn't work if the first person anointed would be healed and the remainder of the thousands in Red Square returned home ill.

All eyes turned towards me as I hesitated to find the words for a response. I was taken aback by the magnitude of this plan, his bluntness, and the thoughtfulness involved that took advantage of every aspect of the consecration for economic gain. This type of thinking would lead to economic success, and soon the Russians would be running the European economy.

I started with the assertion that I didn't perform miracles. It's not a circus act; we don't sell tickets to see it. What happens is that a human being is ill and is suffering immensely. I pray for that person, and then if God grants my request, which is identical to the patient's request, He heals the patient. I cannot guarantee that God will grant my request. I told him that I personally would do whatever he wanted me to do, but it was God who heals. He asked about the healing in Barcelona and how I would describe the power I had. He was missing the point. God raises people from the dead, not me. It's an expression of His power, not mine. He asked about the oil. It was plain olive oil. He asked what happens when the bottle runs out or if the bottle breaks. I told him that as long as a tiny amount of the original oil remained in the bottle, the amount used could be replaced by adding more oil consecrated by the bishop for healing. I had several bottles stored in several places. He could have one of these bottles if he wished. The oil wasn't important. It was merely sued as an outward sign of God's presence. It was a sacramental of sorts. In summary, the oil wasn't important, and neither was I. Both the oil and this human being were used by God. Tomorrow the oil could be lost, and I could be found dead, but the power of God will always remain, and He will find new instruments of His graces.

Gorbachev didn't like my response, especially the part about me dying. He wanted to secure his investment. He asked if I would pray for just two sick people right now. He would be able to see for himself and also be certain that I could cure more than one person at a time. He had missed what I was trying to say. I told him that I would be happy to pray for the sick people but was not sure God would approve of his economic plan. The list was brought in, and he asked me to select two patients. I told him to choose the patients.

One patient had Amyotrophic Lateral Sclerosis (ALS) and was brought into the room. His paralysis was slowly progressing, and he could hardly move his limbs. ALS is sometimes called Lou Gehrig's disease after the great New York Yankee who died from it. The patient's arms and legs were emaciated from severe muscle wasting. He was confined to his bed for the past eight years. The other patient had contractures from severely deforming arthritis. She was bound to a wheelchair, and her limbs were twisted. She could not use her fingers to hold things. When given a cup of water to drink, she compressed the cup between her wrists, brought it up to her mouth, and then returned it to the nurse. Both of these patients were almost forty-five years old.

I started to pray. For the next hour and fifteen minutes, the only sound in the room was my voice and Marybeth's simultaneous translation. I walked up to the man with ALS and anointed his forehead. Then I did the same to the woman in the wheelchair. The man got up from his bed and walked around. Everyone was smiling and watching him. Then he turned to the woman in the wheelchair and helped her up. Her limbs and fingers were straight. She asked for a small coin and proceeded to pass the coin from one hand to the other, grabbing it with her thumb and index finger. The Communists got up and cheered. I was happy for the two patients. Then I asked if I could leave now; the show was over.

"Philip said to him, 'Lord, show us the Father; that is all we need.' Jesus answered, 'For a long time, I have been with you all, yet you do not know me, Philip. Whoever has seen me has seen the Father. Why, then, do you say, 'Show us the Father? Do you not believe, Philip, that I am in the Father and the Father is in me? The words that I have spoken to you do not come from me. If not, believe because of the things that I do. I am telling you the truth: whoever believes in me will do what I do – Yes, he will do even greater things because I am going to the Father. And I will do whatever you ask for in my name so that the Father's glory will be shown through the Son. If you ask me for anything in my name, I will do it. (John 14: 8-14).

CHAPTER 51

EPILOGUE

I<small>T IS NOW TEN</small> years after the day when I first visited Moscow. Mr. Gorbachev and the Communists are wealthy Capitalists now. Everything that "they" planned for the consecration of Russia to the Immaculate Heart of Mary went according to "their" schedule. The world realized it was saved through the intercessions of Mary. Everywhere people were going to confession, praying the Rosary, and receiving communion. Mary no longer appears to the visionaries in Medjugorje, But there was a great sign there. The moment the Pope consecrated Russia in union with the bishops, there was a huge stone heart encircled by thorns with a sword through it that appeared in the ground. It was forty feet in diameter. Below the heart was the word MIR, which means peace in Russian.

I moved back to Boston and have four children now: James, Paul, Peter, and John. They each have blond hair and hazel eyes. Neither of them sleeps much. They are all smarter than I am, and the CIA has promised not to recruit them. I married the ideal woman. At first, after the consecration, I thought that both the CIA and KGB coerced her to marry me. But that made little sense because the day following the consecration, when ninety-one thousand sick people were miraculously cured, the grace of healing that was given to me was taken away. It's just as well. The children need a normal life. My family and I would have been hounded by the public. Marybeth and I were married two years after the consecration when it was obvious that I was a has-been. I spend my summer days driving to the ballpark and rooting for the Red Sox, the New England Red Sox. I built a stadium in Rhode Island that was identical to Fenway Park, with a short, high left-field wall and a screen above it. When you're at the game, you think you are back in Boston. The Boston fans drive over the border to attend the games. They are the greatest fans in the world, and now they are rooting for the World Champion, New England Red Sox. The Red Sox have won the World Series twice in a row. Who would have believed?

Psalm 91

"Whoever goes to the Lord for safety, whoever remains under the protection of the Almighty, can say to him,

"You are my defender and protector. You are my God; in you, I trust."

He will keep you safe from all hidden dangers and from all deadly diseases.

He will cover you with his wings; you will be safe in his cares; his faithfulness will protect and defend you.

You need not fear any dangers of the night or sudden attacks during the day, or plagues that strike in the dark,

Or the evils that kill during the daylight.

A thousand may fall dead beside you, ten thousand all around you, but you will not be harmed.

You will look and see how the wicked are punished.

You have made the Lord your defender, the Most High your protector, and so no disaster will strike you, no violence will come near your home.

God put his angels in charge of you to protect you wherever you go.

They will hold you up with their hands to keep you from hurting your feet on the stones.

God says, 'I will save those who love me and will protect those who acknowledge me as Lord,

When they call to me, I will answer them.

I will rescue them and honor them.

I will reward them with long life; I will save them."

This book was written in the 1980s and had a copywriting in 1990. Many but not all of the events described before that date occurred, as depicted in this novel. Many additional supernatural events occurred that were not included. All of the events after 1990 were fictitious but followed an inspired plot. All references to people such as President Gorbachev, Vice President Quale, President Bush, Pope John Paul II, Cardinal Law, Cardinal O'Connor, James Baker, etc., were fictitious. It was not the intention to injure the reputation of anyone mentioned in the book.

INDEX OF BIBLICAL QUOTATIONS

Subject	Reference
Annunciation	Luke 1: 36-37
Flight to Egypt	Matthew 2: 13-15
Jesus drives out the money changers	Mark 11: 15-18
Peter says he will not deny Jesus	Matthew 26: 33-35
Arrest of Jesus	John 18: 10-11
Jesus appoints Peter	John: 15-17
Paul describes himself	Galatians 1: 11-18
Jesus' love for Jerusalem	Luke 13:34
Denying Jesus	Luke 12: 8-10
Lord's prayer	Matthew 6: 9-13
Protection from the Evil One	John 17: 13-15
Paul's conversion	Acts 22: 6-11

The doubting of Thomas	John 20:25
Jesus appears to Thomas	John 20: 26-27
Definition of love	1 Corinthians 13: 4-8
Praying for healing	James 5: 13-20
Jesus changes water into wine	John 2: 3-9
Ask in the name of Jesus	John 15: 12-17
Parable of the sower	Matthew 13: 3-23
Jesus heals a blind man in stages	Matthew 8: 22-25
The lost son	Luke 15: 11-32
Peter heals a man and raises Tabitha	Acts 9: 31-42
The suffering of Paul	2 Corinthians 11:24-25
The agony of Gethsemane	Mark 14: 32-36
The difficulty of the rich getting to heaven	Luke 18: 24-27
The Transfiguration	Matthew 17: 1-9
The request of James and John	Mark 10: 35-45
The temptation of Jesus	Luke 4: 1-13
The baptism of Jesus	Matthew 3: 13-15
Matthew is called to follow Jesus	Matthew 9: 9-13
The Beatitudes	Matthew 5: 3-12
Persevere in prayer	Matthew 15: 21-28
Jesus raises Jairus' daughter	Luke 8: 49-56
Jesus heals a man born blind	John 9: 1-34

Jesus raises the widow's son	Luke 7: 11-16
Ask in the name of Jesus	John 14: 8-14
God, My Protector	Psalm 91

Good News New Testament and Psalms (Today's English Version. Fourth Edition)
American Bible Society, New York 1976.